Progressive Secular Society

And Other Essays Relevant to Secularism

Tom Rubens

SOCIETAS
essays in political
& cultural criticism

imprint-academic.com

Published in the UK by Societas
Imprint Academic, PO Box 200, Exeter EX5 5YX, UK

Published in the USA by Societas
Imprint Academic, Philosophy Documentation Center
PO Box 7147, Charlottesville, VA 22906-7147, USA

ISBN 9781845401320

A CIP catalogue record for this book is available from the British Library and US Library of Congress

Contents

Preface

i

While varying in subject-matter, this group of short essays does have a focus topic: mechanistic naturalism. The topic is established early in the text, first by the essay 'A Provisional Ontology' and then by the essays 'Appraising Energy' and 'Plato, Shakespeare and Energy'. Supported by references, principally to the physicist Heisenberg, but also to the philosophers Spencer, Nietzsche and Santayana, I contend that energy can be regarded, at least provisionally, as the universe's fundamental substance, i.e., as that which persists through all physical change in the cosmos. Hence my position becomes that of mechanistic energism.

I should add that, in my first book, *Minority Achievement in an Evolutionary Perspective* (1984), I argued for a matter/energy ontology. In my second, *Spinozan Power in a Naturalistic Perspective* (1996), I opted for a more general physicalist position, without pursuing foundational terminology. This latter position is now replaced by one that is specifically energist, though, to repeat, provisional only.

In postulating an energist ontology, I cannot help thinking of a most prescient statement made in the 1940s by the playwright Arthur Adamov. He said that—God being dead—we are on the threshold of an era of impersonal aspects of the absolute.[1] If one regards the 'absolute' as fundamental substance, in the way defined above, then energy can be seen as this absolute. Also, the energist argument can be viewed as the most scientifically cogent of those emerging from the era which Adamov said was beginning (at least for Western man) in the 1940s. It is of course true that ontologies devoid of the concept of a personal deity, indeed of any kind of deity, pre-date the era of which Adamov spoke; in fact, in the most advanced Western thought, such ontologies have been dominant since the late nineteenth century (see, for example, the above references to Spencer, Nietzsche and Santayana). However, Adamov's point can be most profitably taken to be that ontology minus the notion of personal deity would become *the norm* in Western thought, the common currency of all thinking people in Western culture, as

[1] See Martin Esslin, *The Theatre of the Absurd* (1961), in Pelican Books edn, 1976, p. 93.

distinct from being adhered to only by the most advanced minds. It is generally true to say that, over the last half century, this has happened. Despite various kinds of religious revivalism in the West, on balance the position is that most thinking people derive their ontology from empirical science, or at least look to the latter as their ontological starting-point. Science leaves little space for theism, and what little there is is narrowing all the time.

ii

Finally, the essays were written over the period 2002 to the present. This explains why, in the essay 'Reflections on the Resurgence of the Left', I refer to events in 2002 and 2003 as if they were very recent or current. That they are, of course, no longer so is a fact the reader will, I trust, make due allowance for.

T.R., November, 2007

Progressive Secular Society

This text is reproduced by kind permission of the editor of the journal *The Ethical Record*.

A progressive secular society can be broadly defined as one committed to the widening of scientific knowledge and humane feeling. It is based largely on the following humanistic tenets – that man is a part of physical nature, from which he cannot extricate himself; that there is nothing supernatural, i.e. nothing which is not part or product of physical nature, and therefore nothing which science cannot in principle describe; accordingly, that no supernatural agencies (e.g., gods) exist to aid or support mankind; that humanity must therefore be self-sustaining, expecting help from no quarter of the universe (except possibly from areas in which other natural beings of equal or greater intelligence exist); finally, that man's moral perspectives are entirely his own creations and, as such, are, as far as we know, the only available bases for ethical judgement.

In all these respects, secularism makes the human context almost completely self-referential (almost, because of the possibility that intelligent beings may exist beyond the planet). The emphasis on self-reference is a point of central importance in the ways secular society functions, and in the ways its members relate to each other. Secularists see society – all its relationships and activities – as ship on an ocean which perhaps contains no other vessels, certainly no others in sight; as a ship, then, which must ply its course alone if necessary, and, again if need be, look to no one but its crew for the prosecution of that task. At the same time, the crew are not only functionaries; they – or at least a significant number of them – do more than man ropes and watch compass dials. Just as important as these activities are: their perception of the vastness of the sea that surrounds them; their appreciation of each other as comrades; and their enthusiasm for the songs sung along the decks and in the rigging, in all weathers.

The essential character of the secular social project, hinging as that does on both science and humaneness, is to promulgate the scientific attitude in the ontological sphere, and liberal-humanist attitudes in the spheres of ethics and the arts. As the secular mind-set increases in influence, individuals—especially those of highly constructive outlook—view each other as the only available source of support in the effort to achieve social goals and a specific quality of life. Similarly, they look to each other for general enlightenment, clarification, edification. Such expectations may not always be fulfilled, but they are seen as having no other channel for fulfilment. So, increasingly, the search for satisfaction takes a human route, and seeks some kind of human exchange—of thoughts, feelings, actions. More and more, seats are sought at the table of the human symposium, where the perspectives offered claim only human origin. This general tendency is, and has always been, foremost in scientific discourse; but it becomes predominant in the humanities as well, with supernaturalistic terminology receding, especially in the discussion of moral and artistic genius.

Underpinning the whole process is a sense of the tremendous, and perhaps peerless, complexity of the human sphere. The secular humanist views that sphere as the product of a gratuitous evolutionary explosion, one evidencing the staggering plasticity of physical nature. This explosion has shot out a rainbow-cascade of energies, capacities and aspirations, plus associated problems. The cascade is seen as richer than any superhuman realm postulated by supernaturalists, and as having the additional merit of being unquestionably real. Its richness, located as it is in such a small area of the universe, is regarded as meriting no less study than the stellar galaxies—indeed more, if nothing in interstellar space contains phenomena of comparable complexity.

At the same time, different degrees of brightness within the cascade are acknowledged. While the full spectrum of human capacity is deemed superior in quality to the spectrum of any other animal species, there is also the observation that wide qualitative diversity exists within it: ranging from the sub-average to the absolutely outstanding. For the secularist, this observation carries no embarrassing implications: a naturalistic and evolutionary view of man fits seamlessly with the fact of natural inequality in ability, and with the requirement to adjust expectations to that fact. The secularist position is not burdened with compunctions against long-term—indeed, ultimate—appraisal of the individual, unlike those religious doctrines which hold that all human beings are the creation of a divine parent, and are therefore ultimately subject only to divine appraisal.

Secularism openly and explicitly claims ultimate status for human judgements.

However, it insists that such judgements should be as broad-minded and finely-tuned as possible. Hence secular appraisal at its best is a long way from being rigidly conventional and orthodox. It is essentially more sympathetic to individual variety and complexity than any theistic (therefore deo-centric) doctrine could ever be. Being without a superhuman point of moral reference by which everything human is judged, it has a uniquely capacious sense of human variety, of what may constitute self-fulfilment and self-achievement, and of ways an individual may regard himself as a success or failure. The intricacy of this approach is such that certain conventional criteria of success—for example, economic and professional status—are accompanied by many others, and sometimes eclipsed by the latter.

The multiplicity of criteria, or at least of candidates for criteria-status, indicates the secularist's fundamental orientation toward moral debate. Secularism, in the West, is successor to a religious culture that is largely in decline, and this will be its future role in any part of the world where religion is in the descendant. Given this role, it is acutely aware that the moral certainties of the religious mind can never legitimately be resurrected. It also sees that the future of mankind, to the extent that this future is secular, is one from which moral controversy will never be absent. Controversy is viewed as a factor man must learn to live with: the inevitable concomitant of the moral non-objectivism and inter-subjectivism which rises as theistic religion falls. Theism always avers that it possesses objective knowledge of what is good or evil, usually in equal measure to its claim to possess objective knowledge of the existence of deity. The collapse of the latter assertion means the collapse of the former; and objectivity in ethics surrenders the stage to inter-subjectivity, the effort to achieve communal consensus, and to the unparalleled complexities this entails.

In the moral debate on which secular society embarks, discussion of the degrees to which people genuinely communicate with each other is an integral feature. The discussion is frank and unevasive, as indeed it has to be, given the demise of the theistic perspective and therefore of the view that all human beings, as creations of an all-wise deity, are capable of unlimited communication with each other. Extensive experience, contradicting this view and supported by the naturalistic perspective, places the moral obligation of honesty and realism on the secularist, in his consideration of how far people are actually capable of understanding each other: a consideration central to discourse on how they should interact with each other. Though the secularist sees society as a ship, he recognises that not all crew members possess to the same degree the capacities for circumspectness, large-hearted comradeship and cultural appreciation. He knows that not all will shine in these respects, or, for that matter, when storms and emergencies come. Hence the possibilities for magnanimous sharing vary: a fact which is bound to shape how people approach each other, the way of speaking they employ, and the extent (if any) to which they reveal their inmost selves.

Problems of communication, linked as they are to disparities in depth of mind, point to an issue which is a more pressing one in secular society than in any other: the incumbency on the individual of forging a viable ontological outlook. This issue is clearly less prominent in religious culture, where the individual is presented with an established ontology and is expected, with perhaps some qualifications and modifications, to accept it. Here, little is philosophically incumbent on the individual *qua* individual. But in secular society the position is completely reversed, the individual being under total obligation to develop a fully thought-out ontology, or rather as fully worked out as the current state of scientific knowledge permits: one based therefore on science, but also on logic; hence one that can be defended without reference to any assertions which lie outside these two fields.

Secular society, then, foregrounds the issue of individuals' meeting, or failing to meet, their intellectual responsibilities.[1] In so doing, it highlights the communication problem which exists between those people who are endeavouring to measure up to philosophical requirements and those who are not. As regards the latter, the question of whether they are fundamentally capable of long-range intellectual effort is an additional point to consider.

This secular emphasis draws attention, far more so than in religious culture, to the experience of mental struggle, perplexity, uncertainty, even isolation. Such experience is inevitably more extensive in secular society than in religious, for the reason already given: that secularism does not offer the individual any ready-made outlook to be accepted automatically. Secularism calls on the indi-

---

[1] It is true that secular society does not, at all cultural levels, emphasise this issue; but it definitely does at the most demanding of these levels, where respect is accorded to those who make a worthy philosophical effort, and withheld from those who do not.

vidual to construct rather than receive; and to look for his building materials only in (to repeat) science and logic. It is no surprise that, in Western culture, where secular thought is most widespread, the experience of painful ontological questing[a] is a major theme, and has been so for about 150 years—roughly the period of religion's decline in the West. A similar pattern is to be expected in any future culture, anywhere in the world, which witnesses the same decline.

Also, secularism offers the individual no guarantee against a degree of ultimate loneliness. In this, it again contrasts with theistic religion. The latter, for all its concern with individual predicaments, does and, indeed, must offer the individual that guarantee, given its postulates that all human beings share divine parentage, and that all can equally avail themselves of the ontology which confirms deity's existence. Secularism, claiming no complete ontological certainty, and affirming only that it is engaged in a knowledge-building project, can offer no definite or final relief from a quantum of isolation which may be experienced by individuals involved in the knowledge project. Hence, even the heartiest shipmates may contain within themselves certain areas of thought and feeling which they cannot share with each other; just as they may also contain certain areas of pain. This consideration lends additional force to Ortega y Gasset's famous saying that each person is a point of view directed at the universe.

The secular position therefore entails many difficulties (ones, incidentally, which cannot be resolved merely by the attainment of economic prosperity). These difficulties are so numerous that one might be tempted to think that perhaps a religious culture is preferable after all. But this temptation belongs only to weak moments. It is overcome with the renewal of positive response to whatever is challenging, rigorous, and requiring a sense of reality and responsibility. Nothing meets these criteria better than the secular view—still provisional, but thus far in accordance with the findings of science—of man as part of a biosphere which is unplanned and in this sense chaotic; the biosphere being, in turn, part of a universe which is equally unplanned and chaotic. This view, until and unless disproven, incurs multiple demands. It calls for man to abandon the notion that he possesses a cosmic destiny; and to regard the human context as a part of the chaos, as just one momentum (or collection of momenta) amid myriad others in the cosmos, none of them privileged or containing any intrinsic, discoverable significance. Consequent on these requirements is the further one that man acknowledge the full force of the argument against moral objectivism: that he understand that moral values are not to be discovered in the physical chaos surrounding the human mind; rather, that they are—have indeed always been—created by that mind.

Grim though these various implications may be, they firmly anchor the psyche to the present state of scientific knowledge, and compel the realisation that humanity must construct moral significance, since there is none to be discovered, or supplied by the only kind of objective knowledge that exists—scientific. And with this realisation, the head that drooped in defeat at comprehension of cosmic chaos will lift itself again. In other words, man can be fired by the challenge to become consciously a moral creator—to become, in a continually aware way, what he has in fact always been, though in the past usually unconsciously (because influenced by religious culture). Perhaps he will be the only such creator the universe will ever know. To the person with a strictly scientific ontology, the spur to fashion a secular ethical order is perhaps stronger than any other.

Such order, however, because based on moral decisions and choices rather than discoveries, can never be wholly permanent. This point clearly links with what was said previously about the on-going character of moral controversy in secularism. Decisions and choices always have causes and contexts, and many of these factors change: as is testified by the study of global history, and by the cultural diversity of the present-day world. Mutability would of course not obtain if ethical outlooks were really based on discoveries of what is right and wrong. Were the latter the case, the good, once discovered, would always be known as good, just as the discovered composition of the water molecule remains its composition and a fixed object of knowledge. This observation further undermines the claims to objective moral knowledge made by religion.

While stressing moral mutability, we should at the same time acknowledge that changes in moral codes and outlooks are not always total. For example, honesty and truthfulness have been, and still are, more or less universally praised. On this, three things can be said. Firstly, praise of probity is still a matter of deciding, not discovering, what is good. Secondly, while the universality of such praise may well point to certain enduring features in the human psyche (as manifested in human evolution thus far), this still does not mean that a 'discovery' of the good has been made: because what we are looking at is a *psychological* fact about mankind, a fact incurred by man's evolutionary trajectory. Psychological facts explain why man has moral attitudes, but the facts do not justify the attitudes, and therefore provide no basis for claiming moral 'discoveries'. Thirdly, while the valuing of probity persists, other values not in conflict with it emerge in the process of social and cultural change.

Secularism's understanding that large areas of morality mutate has political, as well as general moral, ramifications. Just as no moral system is completely permanent, so is no political; political systems too have causes and contexts, and are to a large extent the product of time and place. The secularist's possession of this insight means that progressive secular society must be, by definition, politically flexible, essentially liberal in character: as open-minded politically as it is scientifically, and always ready to adopt an analytical and historical approach to expressions of political attitude.[2]

However, though ways of thinking about politics must always be contextualist, politics still assumes in secular society an importance it cannot have in religious culture. That importance is bound up with the secular view of man as moral creator. At the political level, this role must include debate on the viability of government's assuming, in certain circumstances, the power of life and death over other human beings. Overall, the political sphere becomes a pivotal area of moral thought and action. While expressing a moral perspective (at least ideally), it knows that the latter is not a discovery, and its passions and dedications are maintained or modified in the light of that knowledge. The secularisation of politics has gradually become predominant in the West since 1789, and this process is reflected in Thomas Mann's famous saying, 'In our time, the destiny of man presents its meaning in political terms.' It is also evident in the way political activity is seen as a locus of moral anguish: for example, in the writings of Jean-Paul Sartre. This perspective on politics can be expected to emerge wherever else in the world the secular mentality develops.

Returning to the over-arching point about mutability in human culture, this understanding of changeability is of course consonant with having a general evolutionary perspective; but even so, many people still find the idea of profound cultural change, involving say a century or so, harder to adjust to than the idea of biological mutation, involving millions of years. Progressive secularism should endeavour to make the former notion less difficult to accommodate;

---

[2] The fact that political attitudes always have a context does not, of course, invalidate them. We are simply drawing attention to context as an inevitable shaping factor.

while, concurrently, possessing a sense of great traditions, of attitudes and activities which have stood the test of time and have, thus far, deservedly retained their adherents. Certain moral and artistic achievements clearly fall into this category.

A major role for the great mind in secular culture is, in fact, to make value-judgements on what should and should not be retained. These judgements must of course be argued for, since no moral knowledge is being claimed; but cogent arguments have to be advanced and debated.

Many of these arguments will centre on the arts, which, in the secular context, assume a greater importance than is possible in religious culture. Not that art has played no important role in religion; it manifestly has had major significance—as is attested by, for example, the architecture, painting and music inspired by Christianity. However, religious art, by definition, always points beyond itself, to a belief-system which is the ultimate source of edification. In this sense, art has a secondary status in the religious context. By contrast, art in the secular context is an ultimate source of satisfaction: it is not a step on the way to something more capacious than itself, is not a point of entry into an all-embracing system of beliefs. In this way, secular art is entirely self-supporting, a goal rather than a path, an end in itself.[3] Thus the position it occupies in the secular framework is primary and foundational. Its shift from secondary to primary status, which Western culture has effected over roughly the past two centuries, will be found wherever progressive secularisation occurs in the future.

However, it may be objected that there is at least one example of art which, despite being secular, held secondary status: the 'socialist realist' art of the former Eastern bloc countries; it was secondary to, because an expression of, a political ideology. The objection is valid, but it only leads us to consider the nature of art which claims to be secular in the fullest sense. Surely such an art must be genuinely empirical, a record of actual, lived experience, and not a construct based on received ideas. The latter, many would argue, was the case with socialist realism; it was not truly empirical because not open-minded, and therefore not progressive. Further, it was relatively short-lived.

---

[3] For a representative twentieth-century expression of this view of art, see W. B. Yeats's lines from *The Tower* (sec. III): 'I have prepared my peace / With learned Italian things / And the proud stones of Greece.'
See also the view of another twentieth-century poet, Wallace Stevens, on the supreme status of creative imagination.

Art's special place in secular culture as an ultimate locus of inspiration and sustenance carries a number of implications. Firstly, the inspiration can be moral as well as aesthetic; no circumspect person would wish to claim for the work of art, especially the literary work, a solely aesthetic value. Secondly, different people find nourishment in different things. Orientation to art is varied and heterogeneous, unlike the homogenous orientation to a belief-system in religion. Such heterogeneity, like moral controversy, is something all secularists must learn to live with, no matter how strong their personal likes and dislikes in art may be. What can make such diversity not only tolerable but also positively stimulating is, clearly, openness to new things, to new ways of responding (both to what is actually novel and to what is traditional but previously un-encountered). In this and other ways, art becomes a region in which various places of not only stimulus but also rest and repose are found. (See again the Yeats quotation.)

Thirdly, value is placed on creativity as such; this is distinct from creativity in the service of religious belief. Provided it is of high quality, sheer artistic fecundity wins a kind of admiration among secularists which is not found among religious believers, because such fecundity is seen as its own justification. The same point applies to originality and experimentation. This admiration may well be linked to the naturalistic basis of the secular outlook; perhaps a parallel is being seen between artistic and biological fertility.

The common responses that art can produce are one form of emotional sharing that secular society can experience. Such sharing is vital for any society, but particularly for the secular kind, given the absence, in the latter, of the specific kind of cohesion which comes with religious allegiance. In fact, a major task for secularists is to achieve a form of widespread mutuality (though this cannot be total) which serves as a viable alternative to that offered by religion. The task is clearly connected with secularism's moral and cultural concerns. Success in it is imperative, since failure will lead many people to relinquish their commitment to secularism and lapse into religion, chiefly in search of a communality of feeling which non-religious society has not provided. A secular communality must of course be bound up with an outlook which is compatible with the current state of scientific knowledge. Given the latter's complexity, the striving for emotional sharing entails many difficulties, far more than those encountered in religious culture, where the current state of science is usually either ignored or seen through the lens of dogma. All the more significant, then, is success in such striving.

Failure, on the other hand, could mean either (as said) a regression to religion or a secular social order that was merely technocratic and functionalist: nothing more than a collocation of discrete technical/occupational activities, none of which, in themselves, guaranteed communality of feeling—or, equally important—philosophical dialogue. Such a society would be free of religious control or influence, yes, but the freedom would be negative: the absence of both what is not needed and what is.

If all else failed, the requisite mutuality could well arise from the sense, previously referred to, of shared species adventure and exposure in a cosmic wilderness where moral order can only be made, not found. This sense, if deeply felt by a sufficient number of people, could be the saving factor which prevented society from becoming excessively atomised.

However, that the communality would not be total is a point which returns us to what was said earlier about communication problems between individuals operating at different intellectual levels. These problems are connected with another: that of mental sub-averageness. This in turn connects with the problem of extreme mental defectiveness. The latter can be defined as total, or near-total, inability to be self-accountable and intelligently self-directing, and therefore inability to make any kind of positive contribution to society. Intractable difficulties—psychological, social and economic—would be entailed by a radical increase in extreme defectiveness; they would include, in some cases, virtually limitless tribulation that the defective would inflict on himself and those close to him. These are problems which every secularist should frankly recognise. Progressive secularism has no choice but to be eugenic in outlook if it wishes to avoid or at least minimise such difficulties. It has no option but to think and act eugenically, seeking, as far as it reasonably can, to ensure that the genetic quality of the population does not too steeply fall below a certain level. To this end, it should advocate the fullest possible research in pre-natal medicine, to find means of accurately predicting the advent of extreme defectiveness, so that appropriate advice and counselling may be given to prospective parents.

Measures to prevent degeneration are part of the secular project to maximise the competence, effectiveness and constructive contribution of all members of society—in other words, society's dynamism and capacity to stimulate and inspire. Society must have this capacity if it is not to be a constriction on the energies and abilities of individuals, if it is not to be merely a formula for conformism and imitation. The aim is for the social whole to be, as far as possible, an outlet for energy rather than a block on it and a dead hand.

In the effort to create such a social reality, the secularist values every collective gain in rationality, co-operation, co-ordination and fluency: everything which brings sun-bursts to the social scene and renders it both technically and aesthetically satisfying. Thus affected, that scene invites the contemplative gaze and induces calm: in the way small townscapes do, as backdrops, in classical painting. Much edification is to be derived from this environmental achievement and fashioned symmetry: things which are then bequeathed to future generations. The geometries of constructed environment are as much a creation as the moral orders which inhabit them; and through them the individual may wander and imbibe, absorbing the dimensions of what will outlive him.

In fact, the sense of what will outlive him is, to the secularist, a general one, applying to many things in addition to environment. His sense differs from that of the religious believer, at least of the believer who subscribes to the notion of a soul and its after-life. Eschewing this notion, the secularist holds that his existence is physical and once-only in character, and that everything else must be seen as part of this perspective. Transience and total extinction are accepted, the more emphatically because the contingent factors surrounding birth are acknowledged. That acceptance grows in steadfastness as the years advance; and attention focuses, with increasing strength, on constructive and creative activity within the space which transience leaves room for. No hopes or expectations lie beyond that space, and those within it are bound up with the aspiration of leaving a moral and/or cultural legacy. This overall position, shared tacitly or otherwise by all secularists, steadies their path across the decades: for as far as that path—a route of courage—threads night-bounded day.

Endnote

[a] This questing, in relation to modern literature, has been poignantly characterised by the literary critic Irving Howe. He speaks of 'a cluster of assumptions central to modernist literature: that in our time men wishing to be more than dumb clods must live in permanent doubt and intellectual crisis; that for such men, to whom traditional beliefs are no longer available, life has become inherently problematic; that in the course of their years they must face even more than the usual allotment of loneliness and anguish ... that courage, if it is to be found at all, consists in a readiness to accept pain while refusing the comforts of certainty.' See *Thomas Hardy* (London: Weidenfeld and Nicholson, 1966) pp. 134–5.

A Provisional Ontology

This text is reproduced by kind permission of the editor of the journal *The Ethical Record.*

Generally, ontologies postulate that total reality possesses a fundamental substance. I am defining total reality as the universe/cosmos. Fundamental substance can be described as that which remains the same throughout all changes, and in this sense 'stands under' ('substans') all mutability. Also, since, for me, total reality contains physical objects (e.g., planets and stars), ontological idealism—the view that reality is entirely mental in character—is ruled out. Hence I can speak of substance as something which, like the physical objects referred to above, exists independently of any consciousness of it (whereas, in ontological idealism, nothing exists independently of consciousness).[1] I can also speak of it as something which is distinct from what it may appear to be to any consciousness.

The ontology I am proposing postulates energy as the universe's foundational entity: energy, then, not just as a characteristic of physical processes but as a physical *thing*, entity. Further, this thing is not only foundational. In the physical sphere—by implication, the foundational sphere—it is all-pervasive, constituting all physical events, processes and states.

Reference to physical events and processes leads to a further point: this ontology draws no operational distinction between events and content of events. Hence it does not argue that events and processes *in themselves* are fundamental substance. Events are always events *of* an entity; they exist on the same level, so to speak, as their content, not on some deeper level. Therefore, even if we were to say that nothing lies deeper than events and processes, we would have to add that, equally, nothing lies deeper than their content; and the latter is energy.

I hasten to add that the energist position lays no claim to originality, since it is bound up with a view which modern physics has promulgated for almost the whole of the twentieth century: that energy is what all physical entities reduce to, including the structures which have been traditionally called 'matter'. As Werner Heisenberg says in *Philosophy and Physics*:

[1] The precise sense in which this term is being used will be specified later.

> Energy is in fact the substance from which all elementary particles, all atoms and therefore all things are made, and energy is that which moves. Energy is a substance, since its total amount does not change, and the elementary particles can actually be made from this substance, as is seen in many experiments on the creation of elementary particles. Energy can be changed into motion, into heat, into light and into tension. Energy may be called the fundamental cause of all change in the world ... Since mass and energy are, according to the theory of relativity, essentially the same concepts, we may say that all elementary particles consist of energy. This could be interpreted as defining energy as the primary substance of the world.[a]

This ontology, like the position in modern physics on which it is based—like, indeed, all positions which are genuinely scientific—is provisional only. If some physical entity more fundamental than energy is discovered in the future—by, for example, developments in inflationary cosmology theory—then the perspective will change accordingly. As yet, however, the principles of the conservation of energy and of momentum remain unrefuted; hence the energist position holds firm thus far.

A further and crucial point to make is that my position is physicalistic: it postulates that the physical sphere, consisting as it does of energy, is actually the only sphere. The so-called foundational reality is, then, the only reality.

As such, as the totality of all that exists and that has ever existed, it is free-floating, self-standing. Hence it is uncaused, since a cause of its existence would be a factor additional to the totality. Such a factor is, by definition, impossible, as no entity can be additional to totality, to the sum total of all entities.

The physical being all, 'consciousness', and the entire category of mental experience, is actually physical processes and states in the brain. This position is of course what, in philosophy of mind, is called the identity theory, according to which thought-activity is identical with brain-activity, the implication being that mental entities and processes do not exist. Later in the essay, I will in fact use mentalistic terms e.g., 'intellect', 'mind', 'cognition', 'intelligible', but only for linguistic convenience, as a *facon de parler.* In all cases, brain states and processes are what will be meant.[2]

---

[2] And not only in this essay, but in all subsequent ones containing mentalistic language, where I am stating my own viewpoint. This point also applies retrospectively to the previous essay. Incidentally, in answer to those critics of identity theory who claim that human dignity is demeaned by the

Hence, when I speak of energy existing independently of and distinct from consciousness of any kind, what is really meant is energy's distinctness of identity from the false identity constructed by any inadequate attempts at self-cognition which energy itself makes: attempts which are, again, physical. Not all attempts, of course, will be inadequate; in the case of adequate ones, the constructing of false identity does not occur.

To illustrate the above point briefly: consider the familiar case of a person—an energy structure—trying to understand himself and failing to; then trying again, and succeeding. Regarding both efforts: convert the mentalistic language in which this situation is conventionally described into physicalistic language, so that reference is entirely to brain states and processes.

A broad implication of the above points is that, wherever energy achieves self-awareness, indeed awareness of any kind, the cognition is actually energy in a new physical state or process: again, a brain state or process. In this sense, new cognition can be defined as a novel physical fact in the cosmos, a novel state and activity of physical structure; and increasing cognition as increasing change of this kind.

Returning to the distinction between what energy is and what it may appear to be, this is one between, to use traditional philosophical language, the intelligible and the sensible. The intelligible is what can be understood by the intellect, the sensible what can be grasped by the senses. Sub-atomic particles, for instance, are known to exist even though they cannot, even in principle, be seen by the eye (since they are smaller than any optical wavelength). Hence, from the standpoint of the senses, energy[3] does not appear to consist of sub-atomic particles, and it is only by going beyond sense-experience, into the realm of the supra-sensible, that the discovery of these particles can be made. This distinction between the intelligible and the sensible is broadly the same as that made by Bertrand Russell between knowledge by description and knowledge by acquain-

---

argument that man's intellectual, emotional and cultural life is physical states and processes, the question can be asked: why demeaned? Why cannot physical entities be accorded the same value as that ascribed to the mental entities which non-physicalists allege exist? The tendency to assign lesser value to the physical than to the mental or so-called 'spiritual' has been a deep-seated one in our culture, and one influenced, sometimes indirectly, by the long tradition of Christian thought.

[3] Of course, only some kinds of energy do actually consist of sub-atomic particles. Light, for example, does not.

tance: the latter is derived from sense-experience, while the former goes beyond such experience.

Further, returning to the initial definition of substance: energy being that substance, and therefore the thing that persists through all change, change can be defined as re-configuration of energy.

Such re-configuration occurs in space-time. It always has spatial location, and duration. Also, energy cannot be fully described without reference to configuration and structure. Energy always exists in specific forms and structures. Moreover, at the macroscopic level, that of large numbers or aggregates of atomic events, every form derives from a previous one. This clearly accords with the conservation principle: any one structure consists of only a finite quantity of energy, and only that quantity is conserved with the new structure derived from it.

Since every energy entity has a structure, it can only act in ways the structure allows. In other words, organization sets the parameters of potential function. The inanimate and the inorganic cannot, because of their make-up, do what the animate and organic can. Also, within the animate and organic sphere, some structures cannot do what others can.

These differences should be viewed in purely structural and operationalist terms. In other words, it suffices to say that a certain organization enables a certain function, that the structure naturally can/does operate in a certain way by virtue of its make-up. Thus structure constitutes capacity, and is therefore the prerequisite of activity. Since organization is ability, the exercise of ability is organization in action. Beyond these specifications, there is no need for discourse on a structure's so-called 'emergent qualities'.

Another point about these differences is that they constitute *qualitative* diversity among structures. The fact that all forms consist of energy does not mean that the differences between them are merely quantitative—simply more of what is in every respect the same. Form is as important a factor as content. Hence variety of form —producing as it does differences in ability and activity—means qualitative variety. The energist ontology is monistic only in one sense, with regard to content; it is pluralistic with regard to form and its properties, i.e., its capacities.

The range of energy structures is of course staggering: a spectrum from simple to breathtakingly complex which perhaps no single human consciousness will ever circumscribe. The spectrum indicates energy's protean character—and this is a point being made about content, about a common factor present in all forms. Its protean character means that energy can re-configure itself in seemingly inexhaustible ways.

Proteanness, fundamental and irreducible, signifies fundamental chaos: chaos not in the sense that there are no regularities in event-sequences, but that these regularities, interpretable as statistical causal laws, have no purpose or goal. Hence, if the regularities are interpreted as causal, then the causality is mechanistic, not teleological. What, then, exists is order (at least in our experience of the universe thus far), but order without purpose: hence an order within which—indeed, *in accordance with* which—all kinds of clashes and collisions occur between different energy forms.

Man must realize the full implications of the fact that he is situated within this chaos, and has evolved from it. This clearly means not expecting the cosmos to contain any features or tendencies which are intentionally favourable to him. There are obviously cosmic facts which are compatible with human existence (otherwise there would be no such existence), but these are compatible purely by chance, mindlessly.

At the same time, protean chaos, precisely because it can move in so many different directions, can conjure the wondrous. Of this fact, human cultural and moral achievement is proof. Eminence in the arts, sciences and philanthropy is the fruit of physical processes within human evolution. Though these processes, like all others, lack a goal, they can nevertheless be deemed splendiferous. And more: they signify that energy is not only protean but, in being this, fecund in the most gratuitously awesome way. The imagination is beggared in trying to conceive the future marvels of complexity that energy's commotion will accidentally incur, to match or surpass those it has already produced. Human greatness, albeit an unintended effect of aimless process, remains, to human eyes, greatness still.

Greatness combines with variety to give the human sphere its unique character as a spectrum of energy forms. Valuing the exceptional and the various is the basis of a liberal culture; or, more precisely, given the energist ontology, of a secular-liberal culture: one that is entirely naturalistic, humanistic and neo-Darwinian in outlook. In the twentieth century, a number of distinguished writers have articulated this outlook; they include Bertrand Russell, E. M. Forster, John Dewey, Andre Gide and George Santayana. Of these, I would like to quote from the last two. On diversity, Gide writes: 'A society of men will never be perfect unless it can make use of many different forms of activity, unless it favours the flowering of many forms of happiness.'[b] Again on diversity but also on its source, Santayana speaks of 'delight in a [physical] mechanism that can fall into so many marvellous and beautiful shapes, and can generate so many exciting passions'.[c]

This delight points to the kind of naturalism which could arguably be regarded as ultimate: the exultant kind. Exultant naturalism welcomes all constructive originality and creativity, and sees the history of human culture as a vast, many-tinted landscape of creative potential realized thus far.

This landscape includes religious culture. The latter at its best is seen as having been a powerfully poetic and allegorical expression of mankind's moral needs and aspirations; though unwittingly so, since religions made—and continue to make—the mistake of treating ideas which are in fact poetic as being literally, scientifically true. Naturalism clearly looks beyond the kind of allegory-expression which it views religion as comprising; it does so because of its commitment to modes of moral statement which are completely compatible with scientific knowledge. Nevertheless, it values the religious-allegorical mode as imaginatively fertile, and as marking a significant historical stage in the development of moral thought: a stage which actually could not have been of a more advanced nature, given the paucity of scientific knowledge in the periods when religions were taking shape, and indeed in many subsequent centuries.

The best of religious culture and of all cultural phenomena manifest the natural complexity, multiplicity and fecundity which are, for the energist, of paramount importance. The future is seen as one in which further human configurations of energy will break new ground, artistically and scientifically, and perhaps also morally. Also, it may be one in which mankind will make contact with other forms of intelligent energy structure elsewhere in the universe: a contact hopefully leading to fruitful co-operation—hence to a widening, across the cosmos, of the sphere of control exercised by mind over non-mind.

Endnotes

[a] As quoted by Brian Magee in *The Philosophy of Schopenhauer* (Oxford: Oxford University Press, 1983) p. 139n.

[b] *The Fruits of the Earth* (1897), in the Penguin Books edn, 1970, p. 202.

[c] *Reason in Science* (1906), (New York: Dover Publications Inc., 1983) p. 90.

Appraising Energy

In 1884, Herbert Spencer spoke of 'An infinite and eternal energy from which all things proceed.'[a] In 1885, Nietzsche described the universe as 'a monster of energy, without beginning, without end'.[b] In 1900, Santayana, influenced by both Spencer and Nietzsche, wrote: 'We are part of the blind energy behind Nature.'[c] Within, then, the space of sixteen years in the last part of the nineteenth century, three of the word's leading philosophers were naming non-rational energy as the ultimate reality. In so doing, they were attacking theism in virtually all the forms in which religions have postulated it.

In their view of the fundamental ontological status of energy, as the substance of which everything, at least everything physical, consisted, they were anticipating in striking fashion pivotal developments in twentieth-century physics. A synoptic statement by leading physicist Werner Heisenberg, on energy as seen by modern physics, was given in the preceding essay 'A Provisional Ontology', and the reader may wish to re-consult this (p. 13 above).

Returning to the words of Spencer and Nietzsche: viewing Spencer's 'eternal' and Nietzsche's 'without beginning' in the light of Big Bang theory, we can say that, if this theory is correct, energy has existed for as long as time has, the latter having come into existence with the Big Bang.

Referring back to Heisenberg and his authoritative statement: it is reasonable to accept an energist ontology as, to repeat, at least a provisional one. Once accepted, however, this ontology raises questions of value. To re-iterate points made previously: the physical world evinces qualitative differences between its various objects. These differences emanate from the diverse ways in which energy is structured and configured; for example, as biological evolution has shown, different configurations produce different capacities and functions.[1] Hence there is the issue of what attitude(s) to take toward these differences. This issue would of course not arise at all if variations were only quantitative and not qualitative, i.e., if physical

[1] Also, to repeat another point, biological evolution, indeed evolution in all respects since the Big Bang, has been change only in form of energy, and not change from energy-content to some other kind of content.

objects either did not differ in organisation or, while differing, did not possess distinctive attributes resulting from these differences.

The recommendation to be made here is that energy be viewed in contextual terms only: what should be evaluated is the specific configuration, the specific physical object, not what all the configurations and objects have in common. In other words, value should be assigned to form and its properties, not to content in the strictly reductive sense. Just as arbiters in a sculpture competition are required to make different aesthetic judgements about statues all made of marble, so, on a cosmic scale, judgements should be made about the forms energy takes. It will not be enough simply to note that energy is protean; the further step must be taken of appraising the results of that protean capacity. (At the same time, however, the fact that energy *is* protean is itself highly significant, prompting the ontological question of why it should be so.)

As I have argued in the opening chapter on 'Progressive Secular Society', morality is not objective but inter-subjective. Hence the values by which we appraise are not forms of objective knowledge; this point must continually be borne in mind – as must its companion-point, that attitudes/values are feeling-positions. Also, it is reasonable to postulate that values have bio-environmental causes and conditions.

Now, in accordance with what I have said in 'A Provisional Ontology', I contend that the emotional experience from which we forge values, along with all mental and sense experience, actually consists of states and operations of energy (specifically, of cerebral and neural structures). Further, repeating another point from that essay, it can be reasonably inferred that there are statistical laws of physics. From that inference, it can be assumed that energy operates in accordance with those laws. If these points are accepted, it follows that we, as energy structures, evaluate other energy structures in accordance with the laws by which energy as a whole functions. In other words, we cannot stand outside energy, transcend it, when we make judgements about its configurations. In appraising, we operate within the constraints of, in conformity with the operational patterns of, the content whose forms we are appraising. There is, then, law- continuity between subject and object of appraisal.

A final point: in 'Progressive Secular Society' the cosmos, biosphere included, was described as unplanned and so chaotic. This is a view that cannot be evaded, and, in connection with it, Nietzsche's phrase 'monster of energy' bears repeating. The vision of a universe which is in essence a gratuitous pullulation of countless energy structures—inorganic and organic, inanimate and animate—is without doubt a daunting one, at least initially. The onset of this perspective is like a precipice suddenly appearing at one's feet; and for a moment reality may seem a spectacle of madness, with oneself a component of that madness. No small amount of courage is required to keep one's eyes fixed on what one sees. This vision is a vertiginous intellectual inheritance, one which every thinking person is heir to.

Eventually, though, the harshness and the sense of dismay are relieved by a focus on those structures regarded as beautiful, intricate, delicate. These undeniably bring deep emotional edification.[2] Yet it must always be remembered that they are part of an energy totality containing forms and processes which are, from a human standpoint, repellent: for example, viruses and bacteria which destroy human life. The person with an energist ontology must acknowledge that no energy configuration, not even the most attractive, objectively occupies any central, privileged or significant position in the universe; it objectively occupies only a location, filling one space rather than another. Value is something assigned to it externally, by the subjective human evaluator, and not something intrinsic to it.

The edification produced by positive evaluation is in effect the mind's resting place in its traversing of chaos. It is the island found in the heaving ocean: the locus of shelter, stability, joy and celebration; and the place where all creative possibilities may be nurtured, husbanded. The strength of attachment to it is not undermined by the equally strong awareness of its boundaries.

---

[2] A feeling which, incidentally, denotes a 'like to like' response mode: the complex responding positively to the complex, the intricate valuing the intricate.

Endnotes

[a] As quoted by J. A. Hobson in his obituary to Spencer in 'The South Place Magazine' for January 1904, published by London's South Place Ethical Society, Conway Hall, Red Lion Square, London WC1.

[b] In *The Will to Power*, tr. Walter Kaufmann and R. J. Hollingdale, and ed. Kaufmann (New York: Vintage Books, 1968) p. 550.

[c] In *Interpretations of Poetry and Religion* (1900), (New York: Harper Torchbook, 1957) p. 245.

Plato, Shakespeare and Energy

In Plato's *Phaedo,* Socrates says:

> those who really apply themselves in the right way to philosophy are directly and of their own accord preparing themselves for dying and death ... if a man has trained himself throughout his life to live in a state as close as possible to death, would it not be ridiculous for him to be distressed when death comes to him? ... true philosophers make dying their profession ... to them of all men death is least alarming. (62E–68B)

Nearly two thousand years after Plato, Shakespeare, in *King Lear,* has Edgar declare that 'Ripeness is all': the one important thing with regard to death is that we should be ready for it (*King Lear,* V.ii). Edgar's words are echoed by those of Hamlet: 'The readiness is all': to be ready for death is all that matters (*Hamlet,* V.ii).

Edgar is not a philosopher, and neither is Hamlet in any strict sense; yet their views chime with those of perhaps the most famous of all Western philosophers. Also, though Plato believed in the immortality of the soul, whereas there is no evidence that Shakespeare did, their sharing of the basic idea that death should be confronted with courageous equanimity is a fact of pivotal importance. This idea is relevant to us all, whatever our ontologies: it points to an experience we all must face, and face—again, whatever our ontologies—without total certainty. (Absence of certainty on this issue is of course given unforgettable expression by Shakespeare in Hamlet's famous 'To be or not to be' soliloquy.)

The subject of ontology relates to the third item in the essay's title. I have previously argued that energy can be provisionally regarded as the universe's fundamental substance; and that the tremendous physical diversity the universe evinces can be seen as different permutations and configurations of this substance. On this view, the death of living organisms is the transformation of one energy structure to another, given that energy is conserved; and, in the case of human beings and a number of other animals, the change is from a state involving mental and sense experience to one which probably does not.

The energist ontology necessarily emphasises stoicism in the face of death, and in this respect is perhaps closer to Shakespeare than to Plato. However, despite this emphasis, it also celebrates complexity: the complexity of energy organisation which is found in the most highly developed human beings. That the highly complex must perish is unavoidable; but that it actually existed before perishing, that it was achieved by the universe before being extinguished, are facts of arguably greater weight. The reality of having existed cannot be nullified by the termination of existence. Death has no retrospective power over what preceded it: its domain is in fact only a moment in the present, behind which lies a past it cannot touch.

Hence high complexity can be rejoiced in despite its finiteness, and despite the fact that it entails more psychological suffering than falls to the less complex, or the non-complex. Such suffering is the mark of depth, so a kind of distinction. Thus Nietzsche saw human beings in terms of a hierarchy based on capacity for suffering; and, returning to Hamlet, the latter might be regarded as the archetype of mental and emotional travail (therefore a literary creation probably unrivalled in its perennial impact). To value complexity is to value intensity of mental and emotional life, whatever the latter's consequences: complexity is given unqualified endorsement.

Further, that endorsement is of an energy state, form, context: one which carries strengths as well as problems. The problems are actually linked to the strengths (e.g., superior intelligence, wider responsiveness, deeper sensitivity); and are, on balance, outweighed by them. Hence, to Santayana's comment that 'There is tragedy in perfection, because the universe in which perfection arises is itself imperfect,'[a] the energist can reply: 'Perfection brings joy even though it is unique and alone.'

The energist's focus on the complex brings a sense not only of the problematic but also of primordial excitement at the near-hypnotically intricate patterns which energy's loom can weave, at the crystalline networks its mechanism builds. Their beauty is unaffected by their destructibility.

Such excitement, rising to awe, is the stuff of an emotion which may be called religious, if we define the religious outlook as one built around a conception of forces which have created man, which therefore surpass him, and which—again therefore—he should strive to live in harmony with. For the valuer of complexity, these forces are energy's most specialised capacities, the ones that hum in its most expert workshop. They are the powers he regards as the ones which have fashioned him, plus others like him in the present and past, and the ones that will fashion others like him in the future. For him, they are the 'more of the same' to which William James referred when he defined religious experience as that of the individual's perceiving realities parallel with himself but outside him: realities to which he therefore wishes to attach himself. (The Latin word 'religio' means an attachment or bonding.) To the energist, such realities are wholly natural and physical—but, of course, no less potent for being so than any alleged supernatural forces. It is to them he speaks when he voices the words of the Biblical Psalm 139: 'I will praise thee; for I am fearfully and wonderfully made.'

The energist's sense of what physically produced him and transcends him reinforces his stoicism in the face of death. His view is that he has been part of something greater than himself, and that the same applies to others across the time-spectrum. This perspective fully attunes him to the words of Socrates previously quoted.

Endnote

[a] *Reason in Science*, pp. 237–8.

'Great Creating Nature'

Shakespeare and Santayana

For I have heard it said
There is an art which, in their piedness, shares
With great creating nature.

The above quotation is from Shakespeare's *The Winter's Tale* (IV.iv. 87–9). It is one of the poet's many expressions of wonder at the creative capacity of the physical world. Others include: *Cymbeline,* V.iv.48, and *Coriolanus,* V.iii.33, in both of which is found the phrase 'Great nature'.

For the secularist, the sense of the staggering plasticity and dynamism of the physical is ontologically central; and, even though it is tempered by the awareness of nature's unplanned and therefore chaotic character, a character which has, in Tennyson's phrase, a 'red in tooth and claw' aspect as well as one which inspires awe, the latter feeling remains a major component of the secular outlook. Hence early twenty-first-century secularism can imbibe directly from Shakespeare's early seventeenth-century poetic command of fact.

A secularist of the twentieth century who can support us in this activity is George Santayana. Not only was Santayana, like countless others, a general admirer of Shakespeare, but he also wrote an essay on him: 'The absence of religion in Shakespeare'. Not that Santayana is completely uncritical of his subject: he regards the absence of extensive consideration of the religious outlook as a lacuna in Shakespeare's work which prevents it from being that complete picture of human culture which would be inclusively informative to those at a future stage of human evolution, or to intelligent beings on another planet. Nevertheless, Santayana does see Shakespeare's *oeuvre* as 'the truest portrait and best memorial of man', and even says that 'the absence of religion in Shakespeare was a sign of his good sense ... a healthy instinct kept his attention within the sublunary world ...'[1]

In fact, the philosopher's naturalistic outlook, as reflected in his phrase 'the sublunary world', is the predominant factor in his

[1] As quoted in *The Wisdom of Santayana,* ed. Ira Cardiff (London: Peter Owen Ltd, 1964) pp. 188, 190.

response to Shakespeare. This outlook is, by definition, anti-supernaturalistic: it means the replacement of the supernaturalistic approach by the scientific, and the focusing of all positive attitudes on the natural sphere. Thus Santayana writes, in *The Realm of Matter*:

> When the heart is bent on the truth ... science must insensibly supplant divination, and reverence must be transferred from traditional sanctities to the naked power at work in nature, sanctioning worldly wisdom and hygienic virtue rather than the maxims of zealots or the dreams of saints. God then becomes a poetic symbol for the material tenderness and the paternal strictness of this wonderful world.[2]

In the phrase 'naked power at work in nature', Santayana returns us directly to Shakespeare's 'great creating nature'. We can add to this the quotation from *Reason in Science,* previously given in 'A Provisional Ontology', which speaks of 'delight in a [natural] mechanism that can fall into so many marvellous and beautiful shapes, and can generate so many exciting passions'.[3] Modern secularism, as systematic philosophy, joins hands with Renaissance poet's instinctive insight.

---

[2] *Ibid.,* pp. 256–7
[3] *Reason in Science,* p. 90.

Shakespeare's Perennial Impact

A Confirmation of Determinism?

Santayana's previously quoted words on Shakespeare's works—'the truest portrait and best memorial of man'—are of course among many tributes saying more or less the same thing. The tributes are in fact so numerous that one hesitates to quote another, for fear of producing tedium and of giving the impression that one regards that particular plaudit as being either more important or more eloquent than all the others. However, while wishing to avoid giving this impression and producing tedium, I would like to refer to the words of J. M. Robertson, one of the lesser known commentators on Shakespeare— indeed, one of the lesser known but nevertheless major British writers of the late nineteenth and early twentieth centuries. He avers:

> Why else should it be that, while the dreams shift and waver and are transformed from year to year; while what was thought to be everlasting truth crumbles into dust as of vanishing skeletons, men perpetually turn with the same eager interest to this world of immortal imagination, this strange sea of human life, whose waters seem to clothe with a new vitality the bleached bones of the primal man? What can the reason be but this, that here we do get truth concerning life and conscience ... a view of the world-drama in which our own concerns become newly intelligible because we see them as part of the human whole ... he [Shakespeare] has ... revealed us to ourselves.[a]

The pith of both Santayana's and Robertson's statements, and of all others like them, is that people now do not essentially differ from those whom Shakespeare observed and depicted. If indeed there has been no fundamental alteration in human behaviour—or, to modify this position, if *certain leading forms* of behaviour have not changed—then the implication appears to be that these particular forms are deeply ingrained in the human species.

Such a line of thinking inevitably raises the issue of free-will versus determinism. The postulator of absolute and unconditioned free-will might claim that behaviour can be both recurrent and at the same time chosen in a free and uncaused way; so that each generation in each century in each part of the world displays an unconstrained liberty in behaving in exactly the same ways as, it so happens, its predecessors did. On this view, congruity in action, no matter how extensive, is merely coincidental. However, determinists will contest this argument, claiming it is highly unlikely that such prolonged sameness can be just coincidence. They will look to events in nature at the sub-human level, those studied by the 'hard' sciences, and point out that here recurrence, consistency and regularity are normally interpreted causally, as expressions of causal laws. Why, then, they will ask, should not regularity at the human level be viewed in the same way?

Given the argument that certain features of behaviour have remained constant across variations in environment and culture, it can be argued that the causality in question must be a matter of genetic programming. The 'programmed' postulate in relation to human beings is this: genetically programmed behaviour is a sub-set of genetically enabled behaviour. *All* behaviour is genetically enabled, in the sense that it depends on a pre-existing genetic capacity for performance.[1] However, on the environmental side, programmed behaviour of the kind we are associating with Shakespeare's work requires for its performance only a small range of social/cultural stimuli and outlets. (The programmed behaviour being discussed here is obviously of a complex variety, to be distinguished from other programmed kinds which only meet elementary biological needs, such as the securing of food and shelter, and acts of self-preservation.) This behaviour differs from other complex but non-programmed types, in that the latter depend for performance on a wide range of social/cultural conditions. The difference is due

---

[1] This point about pre-existing genetic capacity is pivotal. While it is true that behaviour always results from an interaction between the individual's genetic endowment and his/her environment, that interaction has a specific character, and the character is determined by the genetic component. This must logically be the case; for, when we speak of environmental influence, we speak of response to environment; response can only arise from capacity for response—which, by definition, must be *pre*-environmental. Response-capacity is genetically determined. Hence it is genetic factors which decide the parameters and possibilities of response to environment, and therefore of interaction with environment. In this sense, the genetic component is primary. Environment is secondary, in that it does not create capacity for response. The genetic is the indwelling, the environmental the incoming; without the genetic, the environmental would have nothing to impact on, nothing to be received by.

to the fact that programmed behaviour—of all kinds, but especially the kind we are focussing on—has behind it a much stronger genetic impetus than non-programmed behaviour: so strong that it operates in many different kinds of environment, each environment containing the requisite minimal conditions for its operation.

The postulate of genetically programmed/determined behaviour accords with the compatibilist view of freedom i.e. we are free when we do what we desire to do without being prevented from so acting by factors external to ourselves. At the same time, compatibilism does not say that we are free to choose our desires and aspirations, or, for that matter, our capacities; and the general postulate of genetic conditioning insists that we are indeed not free in these respects. Hence, given Shakespeare's depiction of desires and aspirations, hopes and fears, devotions and aversions—that 'strange sea of human life' with which so many subsequent generations have identified—it can be argued that he was bearing witness to the behavioural results of certain genetic processes which were, given appropriate environment, inevitably to recur, with the same consequences.

If genetic programming does obtain, it follows that we will find today people who, in varying degree, echo Shakespeare's characters. Perhaps we ourselves are part of the echo. This line of reasoning implies that there is a necessity in certain kinds of behaviour, and that, in this sense, the ancient Greek philosopher Heraclitus was correct when he said that character is destiny. That such a thing as character exists, and that it is destiny in the sense that it is the strongest factor shaping behaviour, was a view propounded not only in ancient times but also as recently as the nineteenth century, by Schopenhauer and Hardy. It is noteworthy that the latter two were deeply influenced by both Greek thought and by Shakespeare.[2]

---

[2] Schopenhauer in particular praised Shakespeare for his insight into the character-consistency which people display throughout their lives. On this point about consistency, it can be argued that, while behaviour does change—as a result, for example, of education or wider experience—that change does not signify an alteration in basic character. What is happening is that new experience is awakening previously undiscovered potentiality in the individual, or eliciting desires that s/he either did not feel before or felt in a different kind of way. In all cases, we are looking at the pre-experiential capacities of the individual, capacities to feel and do (see again note 1). These abilities are part of the person's basic character, and are as unchosen as everything else in his/her make-up. Hence novel activity as a result of new experiences is not a change of character but an extension and further unfolding of it. Viewing things in this perspective explains why the individual responds to the new experience in the specific way s/he does,

This underlines Shakespeare's central importance as a point of reference in determinist thinking.

If, then, character-necessity is at work in at least some kinds of behaviour, it would appear that we can do no other than recognise this fact and acquiesce in self. What we cannot change, we have to accept. This position may seem unduly passive, but here two observations can be made. Firstly, character expresses itself in action: 'operari sequitur esse', as the Latin dictum goes. Also, willing, as the basis of action, is a part of character. Willing, or, more specifically, the ability to will and the tendency of willing, are not things acquired externally, from the environment (nor are they to be confused with *stimuli activating* them, which environment unquestionably does provide). Not being an external acquisition, they cannot be taught: 'velle non discitur', as another Latin dictum goes. Hence acceptance of character is acceptance of a certain will-tendency and kind of activity, an endorsement of our most significant propensities and actions as they manifest themselves and unfold. To the extent, then, that it is referenced to action, the acquiescence is not passive. Secondly, as another saying goes, 'Freedom is the recognition of necessity'. We are free only where we know, and to know ourselves—the injunction, of course, of the ancient Delphic oracle—is to possess the freedom for making accurate appraisals and predictions about ourselves, a freedom (and a benefit) from which ignorance would debar us.

However, it may be argued that this way of thinking is all very well in relation to people who echo Shakespeare's commendable and sympathetic characters. But what about people not in this

---

and not in some other way. In this sense, *everything* a person does is consistent with, because it does not go beyond, his/her capacities and make-up.

As a further point on character-consistency, note the twentieth-century work on typology done by Kretschmer in Germany in the 1920s and by Sheldon in the USA in the 1940s. Both reacted against the strongly environmentalist bias of early twentieth-century psychology, including Freudian, and focussed instead on the pre-environmental factors of anatomy and physiology. They sought to define character-types based on correlation between physique and personality. Despite certain differences in their views, their conclusions are in large measure similar, and are of major significance in contemporary psychology.

To stress the importance of pre-environmental factors in shaping behavioural consistency is not, of course, to disregard the role of environmental ones. As said, both play their respective parts. But it must be repeated that environment is secondary: the impact of the incoming is decided by the nature of the indwelling. Genetics sets the limits to the role environment can play.

category—those who are like, for example, Iago or Richard III? This is in fact a question of vital importance, raising as it does the perennially discussed issue of whether people who consistently do what is universally regarded as evil, and do it actually regarding it as evil, act by necessity. Are there, in other words, people of evil *character* who *cannot* act otherwise? If there are, then clearly no valid argument can be advanced for these people's accepting their characters and endorsing the actions arising from them.

The above questions obviously return us to the free-will versus determinism argument mentioned previously. It should immediately be noted that the main monotheistic religions—Christianity, Judaism and Islam—argue staunchly for complete free-will: human evil, they say, is a matter of man's possessing absolute and unconditioned *internal* liberty in both willing and acting—a position which goes well beyond compatibilism. This position is opposed by determinists on a number of grounds, including the following: firstly, actions and volitions which are said not to be effects of causes are totally inexplicable, and to insist on the inexplicable is to be un-scientific. Secondly, even on the view that evil volitions are free, the question arises as to whether there is a causal link between these volitions and the evil actions which follow them. If there is no such link, then the evil action, while free, is hay-wire and groundless in character; whereas in the real world all too many evil actions bear the mark of being willed, of being planned and premeditated. Thirdly, if we seek to interpret human actions in basically physical terms, then the idea of uncaused volition or action, of pure origination, runs counter to the conservation-of-energy principle, one accepted by almost all physicists. Fourthly, theism of the Christian/Judaic and Islamic kind logically requires the postulate of absolute free-will in order to ensure that human evil is not viewed causally. If it were, questions would be raised about causal chains. In that event, the human will might be seen as the cause of evil action (see previous point); in which case the action would not be completely free. In addition, questions would be asked about the cause of the human will's having an evil disposition. Such questions might lead to the suggestion that the cause lay with the Being regarded as more powerful than man or any other existent: God. Hence would arise the paradoxical notion of a deity, both omnipotent and beneficent, who instigates human evil.[3]

Given the case for viewing evil causally, there is a valid argument that certain kinds of wrongdoing are rooted not in social and environmental pressures but in 'character': they are a grossly disproportionate reaction to whatever external pressures may be their context. In this regard, let us look again at Shakespeare's Iago and Richard III as true-to-life creations. Although the destruction they wreak has, as its context, resentment at a particular social situation, that destruction is of enormous magnitude, and undertaken with little or no inner conflict; as a reaction, it goes far beyond what most people who also felt resentment would be prepared to do. These considerations suggest that external pressures triggered processes in the characters' psychology, but that the processes are far more significant than the pressures which prompted them. The implication is that an innate ferocity was stirred, a sleeping monster awakened. If this interpretation is accepted, then the ferocity and the monstrosity must be seen as 'character' factors. And if these factors are regarded as primary, we return to the question of whether Iago and Richard III can help functioning psychologically in the way they do. More precisely, the question is: of all the circumstances containing the normal quota of factors which disaffect human beings, are there any in which these characters' capacity for extreme perversity would not be activated? If the answer to this question is negative, then it seems we are dealing with a kind of inevitability, an inescapable triggering of reaction disproportionate to occasion. If this inevitability is a matter of 'character', then it is also a matter of necessity.

Now, applying this reasoning to people in the real world, the conclusion to be drawn is that we should be continually prepared to encounter certain individuals whose behaviour may constitute an insoluble problem: behaviour which cannot be adequately explained in terms of environment and other external factors, and which cannot be changed by alterations in these factors. As to an adequate explanation, we can for the moment simply ponder a question which Shakespeare himself asks, in the person of King Lear: 'Is there any cause in nature that makes these hard hearts?' For the determinist, there are always causes; and, in the case of persons regarded as naturally evil,

[3] It goes without saying that these four points represent only a fraction of the number of arguments against the postulate of absolute, unconditioned free-will. The literature on determinism is vast: a fact which, here, needs only to be noted. For further treatment of this subject, see later essay, 'Some arguments for determinism'.

they are internal, genetically programmed; but further statements on the subject are beyond the scope of this short essay. Suffice it to conclude by saying that Shakespeare, among the many illuminations he provides, alerts us to the existence of the fundamentally dangerous human being: the person who—as 'character' determinism argues—is what he is not of his own choosing.

Endnote

[a] J. M. Robertson, 'The religion of Shakespeare', a lecture delivered to London's South Place Ethical Society on 10 July 1887, and published in *Discourses No.7*, available at S.P.E.S., Conway Hall, Red Lion Square, London WC1.

Secular Stoicism

As has been said, the individual in even a highly co-operative secular society may carry certain thoughts, feelings and kinds of pain which cannot be shared with others. When this is the case, an ultimate stoicism is called for: ultimate, because the impossibility of sharing with human beings is not transcended by the possibility of sharing with deity—the latter being, of course, no part of the secular outlook. It is in this way that the stoicism of the secularist differs from that of the theist, who is convinced he can look beyond the failures of human communication to unlimited communication with the divine.

Also specific to the theist, at least in the Christian tradition, is the notion of salvation: another belief which makes his stoicism provisional only. He is sure that salvation, in an after-life of the spirit, will deliver him from the predicaments in this life which require endurance; hence that his stoicism will be rewarded. There will, in other words, be an uplifting sequel to suffering, an eventual dispelling of dark clouds by sunbeams. The complete rejection of this perspective by the secularist—a rejection based on the only criteria he regards as viable, those of science and logic—renders his stoicism non-provisional, hence fully-fledged, and in this sense purer than that of the theist.

This fully-fledged character involves courage to the highest degree: courage to sustain predicaments without any hope of immortality[1] and any belief in a transcendental sphere; the courage to continue moral and cultural endeavour in the face of persistent adversity, without prospect of recompense not only in a future life but even perhaps in this one. The robustness of secular stoicism has much to recommend it.

---

[1] This hope, as Schopenhauer among others has observed, constitutes the chief psychological appeal of religious doctrines: an appeal greater than even that of the idea of an all-loving God.

Camus and Modern Secular Tragedy

In a lecture[1] entitled 'The future of tragedy', given (appropriately) in Athens in 1955, Albert Camus argues that tragic drama always emerges in a period when tension exists between a traditional outlook and a radically new one. Tragedy occurs because this tension is not resolved, and the latter is not resolved because each outlook is seen as having its own kind of validity, its own kind of rightness. Where one of the outlooks triumphs and prevails over the other, tragic drama ceases, precisely because tension has ceased.

Camus sees this characterisation as applying, in various ways, to the period of Greek tragic drama from Aeschylus to Euripides (with Sophocles pre-eminent), and to Western European drama (England, Spain and France) in the late sixteenth and then seventeenth centuries. In each case, the traditional perspective was a religious and collective one (polytheism, Christianity), and the new one was a rationalistic and individualistic one. In each period, the latter viewpoint eventually prevailed, and tragic drama ended.

Camus thinks that the modern West is now in the kind of cultural condition which could give rise to a new form of tragic drama. (Though the lecture is half a century old, the word 'now' still broadly applies.) There is a traditional outlook, though not primarily a religious one: the rationalistic optimism inherited from the Renaissance and the Enlightenment. It is in tension with a mood of doubt and scepticism which is a more recent phenomenon, stemming mainly from the traumatic experiences of the twentieth century (principally, two world wars). Each perspective has its own kind of validity: one is a matter of hope, the other of doubt. The latter view regards history as formidably complex and ambiguous in significance, and entailing certain problems which may be insoluble. As Camus says: 'Man doubts whether he can conquer history; all he can do is struggle with it.' (This view is in marked contrast to much historicist doctrine of the nineteenth century, particularly that of Marx.) The former view sees history and human motivation in more straightfor-

---

[1] For the text of the lecture, from which I will be quoting, see *Camus: Selected Essays and Notebooks* (1970), in the Penguin Books edn, 1979, pp. 192–203.

ward terms, and is therefore more optimistically activist. Modern man, says Camus, oscillates between these two positions, and the oscillation, in its extreme form, is between 'absolute hope and final doubt'.

Camus's analysis of the West's cultural condition is, I think, largely correct, and is echoed by a number of thinkers who have questioned the optimistic assumptions of the Enlightenment, in particular doctrines of inevitable and all-embracing progress. These thinkers include Russell, Popper, Santayana, Berlin and Forster. Hence we can agree with Camus that a new form of tragic drama could emerge from the experience of hovering between hope and doubt—or, perhaps, between a position that is predominantly hopeful and one that is predominantly doubtful. The tragic syndrome would presumably be one of hesitancy and indirection, not unlike that of Shakespeare's Hamlet.

This syndrome would be experienced as tragic chiefly by the secularist. Conversely, it would not be seen as at all tragic by those religionists who believe in salvation and an after-life: a tragic perspective is an ultimate one, and no earthly situation, no matter how grim, is viewed by these believers as a *non plus ultra*. Thus, apart from the minority of religionists who do not subscribe to doctrines of immortality, it is secularists who—without exception—regard earthly situations as ultimate.

In considering what new kind of tragic drama could appear, we have of course to be aware that a good deal of modern Western drama already written has been described as tragic: see, for example, Raymond Williams's seminal study, *Modern Tragedy*. There are, clearly, various ways in which the word 'tragic' can be applied to a modern play. What we are specifically concerned with is a kind of play which has a broad philosophical backdrop, as had the tragedies of ancient Greece: this backdrop would be a post-Enlightenment one, essentially humanistic and naturalistic, but bereft of the certainties which underpinned Enlightenment humanism. Those certainties, as Camus indicates, included the view that history could be mastered, i.e., that rational and humane values would come to lead the historical process; and that, by implication, applied science would be wholly beneficent. Modern experience has shown such absolute confidence to be groundless.

A secularism without historical or social certainties,[2] one that feels the gale-force of doubt about fundamental human directions, recognises ambiguity in much human action, and perceives the vast moral variability among human beings: this is the kind which could provide the framework for a certain kind of panoramic modern play, a certain type of modern tragedy.

[2] The absence of these certainties is signified, incidentally, in the rejection of 'grand narratives' by post-modernist thinkers such as Lyotard.

Mechanism

> The aim of the natural sciences is to resolve themselves into mechanics.
>
> *Helmholtz*

In connection with what was said about determinism in the essay on Shakespeare, the general mechanistic viewpoint needs to be examined briefly. Mechanism is synonymous with determinism in contending that all action at the macroscopic level (again that of large numbers or aggregates of atomic events) consists of an unbroken and interlinking series of happenings: that it displays a complete continuity of cause and effect. Hence mechanism assumes the existence of causal laws in the macroscopic sphere; and even though it regards these laws as only statistical and probabilistic (given the abandonment by twentieth-century physics of the classical, Newtonian view that nature behaves in consistent fashion with absolute invariability), it still places the concept of regularity at the centre of its outlook.

To be more precise in definition: the word 'law' is a term we have formulated to *name* the consistencies in nature's behaviour which we have experienced thus far. Hence, to say that laws exist is to say that there exist regularities to which a name can be attached: the latter being the word 'law'. This means that laws are not things existing outside nature and controlling its activity. They are nothing other than the consistent ways in which nature acts, and has acted hitherto. They are, then, nature's modes of behaviour.

Further, it is only if these ways and modes are to be called 'things' that laws can also be called things. But, in considering this line of thinking, one must guard against false reification. A *way* of behaving is in fact only the behaviour, not an entity contained in the behaviour.

(Also, when we speak of 'constraints' imposed by laws on what can happen in nature, we are again referring to consistent event-processes, and stating an assumption that these consistencies will continue. Once more, we do not mean controlling factors operating externally on these processes. The term 'constraint' is strictly to do with our expectations.)

With the demise of the Newtonian position, and its replacement by the view that nature will *probably*, not certainly, display in the future the regularity it has shown so far, our concept of law has become statistical, based on probability. Again, what is being described is our perspective. That perspective, to repeat, hinges on the notion of regularity, but, as we have seen, no longer in the traditional, unmodified way.

Being regularity-based, mechanism can therefore be seen as the most scientific of all approaches to interpreting the world – offering, at least in principle, a completely orderly and methodical description of action and process, one without gaps or lacunae. It presents the fullest account of any specific state of affairs, covering all the factors which led up to it and rendered it what it is. For example, the mechanist will choose a particular sand-grain from a massive dune and explain its size, location, and position in relation to all the other grains in the dune, all in terms of antecedent causal factors. He will do something similar with a single, falling snowflake, or a shred of floating cloud.

Mechanism thus sees all macroscopic process as systemic, as co-ordinated regularity. However, for many mechanists, this regularity is not purposive: order does not imply purpose. Such a viewpoint is actually the predominant one in modern science, which in the main seeks mechanistic explanations of events rather than teleological ones: that is, it looks for an explanation of event B only in preceding event A, as distinct from looking to both event A and to alleged purpose C, a purpose seen as embracing both A and B. In other words, it seeks efficient, not final, causes. The mechanistic view has been the chief hallmark of science in the West since the seventeenth century, differentiating it from the largely teleological/religious outlook which had been dominant till then.

As to the question of how mechanism can bring about novelty, assuming the operation of laws which are at least statistical, a cogent reply comes from Santayana, in *Reason in Science* (p. 77):

> Novelties in the world are not lacking, because the elements entering at any moment into a given combination have never before entered into a combination exactly similar ... The situation may therefore always be new, though produced from the preceding situation by rules ...

This is an effective rejoinder to critics of mechanical naturalism such as Marxists, who argue that mechanical processes could not be genuinely creative, and instead postulate what they call dialectical processes.

In connection with the above points, Santayana avers that a mechanistic outlook gives us an 'instinctive sympathy, a solicitude for the perfect working of any delicate thing, as it makes the ruffian tender to a young child' (*ibid.*, p. 86). With his typically effective use of concrete language, the philosopher drives home the point that mechanism is not only a philosophically viable position but also one deeply satisfying to the emotions.

Regarding what Santayana sees as the priority of bodily mechanism to mental experience, he asks:

> Is it the mind that controls the bewildered body and points out the way to physical habits uncertain of their affinities? Or is it not much rather an automatic inward machinery that executes the marvellous work, while the mind catches here and there some glimpse of the operation, now with delight and adhesion, now with impotent rebellion?[1]

His answers to these two questions are, of course, 'no' and 'yes' respectively.

However, acceptance of the mechanistic argument does not mean an end to all problems to do with explanation; for, if the postulate of statistical law is accepted, at least one question which now arises is: why are these laws as they are? The consistency and regularity designated by the term 'statistical law' stand in need of explanation. This explication cannot, of course, be achieved by referring to laws as the cause of the consistency, since the laws *are* the consistency — that, and not entities existing independently of the consistency as causal agents. Hence the search is for factors producing the regularity synonymous with law. For want of a viable alternative, the mechanist seeks explanation within the natural world, within the sphere that is, in principle at least, open to scientific investigation. This approach may be defined as mechanistic naturalism.

It is to be sharply differentiated from the traditionally 'metaphysical' approach, as definitively articulated by Schopenhauer when he speaks of a kind of knowledge that

> goes beyond the possibility of experience, and so beyond nature or the given phenomenal appearance of things, in order to give information about that by which ... this experience or nature is conditioned, or, in popular language, about that which is hidden behind nature and renders nature possible.[2]

---

[1] As quoted by Will Durant, *The Story of Philosophy* (1947), (London: Ernest Benn Ltd, 1955) p. 423.

[2] In *The World as Will and Representation*, vol. 2, tr. E .F. J. Payne (New York: Dover Publications Inc., 1958) p. 164.

Also, 'metaphysics goes beyond ... nature, to what is concealed or hidden behind it.'[3]

Fundamental to Schopenhauer's argument for metaphysics is the point that purely physical/scientific explanations of events and processes refer to causal laws. But these laws, he goes on to say, depend for their operation on forces of nature, which he contends are 'absolutely inexplicable' and 'inscrutable'. He includes among these forces heat, electricity, chemical forces, elasticity, impact, weight and hardness. He argues that these factors, which make the laws what they are, lie beyond the power of physics to explain. Thus the explanation must be *meta*physical. Schopenhauer marshals this line of reasoning against the claim that there can be an absolute system of physics, therefore an absolute naturalism. The contrary, he insists, is the case: physics can only be relative to metaphysics, and advances in the former only re-shape the questions presented by the latter: 'the most complete [physical] knowledge of nature possible is the corrected *statement of the problem* of metaphysics'.[4]

A nodal point in this argument is the contention that natural forces are beyond scientific investigation. By contrast, naturalism, and the scientific world-view in general, submit that nothing can be said to be beyond such enquiry, simply because there is no way of knowing, at any given point in time, that future investigation is impossible. This point is powerfully reinforced by the plain historical fact that, in the past, many things were said to be inexplicable which, as a result of scientific investigation, turned out not to be so.

Essentially, what is at issue here is whether we can ever know why elemental physical forces exist, and why they are as they are; also, why such factors (if any) which produced them exist. Enormously complex though this subject is, naturalism is justified in pointing to recent research work in physics on fundamental forces and unified field-theory. Also, this work is ongoing, and its yield may be rich. It will not do, therefore, to advance any final commentary on natural forces as 'absolutely inexplicable'.

It is true that the above projects are (or at least attempt to be) *descriptive*: they depict, in increasingly precise ways, *how* things are, as distinct from *why* they are how they are. In this sense, they are open to Schopenhauer's criticism of science in general: that description, no matter how extensive, lacks a metaphysical dimension, i.e., a pervasive explanation of why the 'hows' are of one kind rather than

---

[3] *Ibid.*, p. 183.
[4] *Ibid.*, p. 178.

another. Nonetheless, one could object that metaphysical 'why' assertions are themselves open to criticism, and in the following way. The assertions claim to account for the natural phenomena which science describes, but the metaphysical factors which allegedly determine these phenomena must be postulated as ultimates, since otherwise they stand as much in need of explanation as the phenomena they are supposed to account for. (Indeed, unless they are said to be ultimate, an infinite regress of explanatory requirements opens up—in much the same way as it does with Christianity's 'First Cause' argument for the existence of God.) If, then, this postulate is made, the question then arises of the grounds for making it. What is the justification for claiming that something has no cause, conditions or antecedents?

The difficulties surrounding metaphysical contentions do not necessarily mean that the latter are invalid or nonsensical, but they do point to the formidable problems that arise when attempts are made to move beyond the norms of scientific discourse, especially beyond concepts of law, causality and mechanism. It is only by adhering to these norms that research programmes can be fruitfully conducted into postulates about what exists. Hence the mechanistic naturalist directs his gaze to the areas to which these norms apply, finding other directions unprofitable. While not dogmatically claiming that the natural sphere is absolute—indeed, not dogmatically claiming anything—he doubts the existence of anything to which that sphere is relative. He regards answers to all questions about the structure of reality as most likely to lie ever-deeper down in the region which science mines.

Some Arguments for Determinism

This text is reproduced by kind permission of the editor of the journal *The Ethical Record.*

This paper will present a number of arguments (though by no means an exhaustive list) in favour of the view that human behaviour is continuously caused, so always subject to causal determinism. By the word 'determinism' I therefore mean an unbroken process of causation. Also, I will contrast this determinism with 'libertarianism', the doctrine which claims that certain human actions are not, or not entirely, governed by causality. The libertarian notion of free-will is also referred to as absolute free-will, in contrast to a concept of relative free-will, involving causation, which I will discuss later.

However, before proceeding with the arguments, something needs to be said about the whole conception of causation. Most present-day determinists accept Hume's view that the notions of cause, causal linkage and causal law are interpretations of the fact of regular conjunction between particular events—or rather of the regular conjunction experienced thus far. They are interpretations because they are not what we see; what we see is conjunction only. Nevertheless, though interpretations, they are seen by determinists as having more than a purely psychological significance. This was all they had for Hume, who regarded them as simply products of the mind's habitual way of trying to make sense of its experience of the external world. By contrast, determinists view them as the most reasonable way of comprehending the fact of regular conjunction; and —taking a crucial further step—as therefore providing a legitimate basis for postulating that causality actually exists. This postulate then becomes a working hypothesis, though one always wedded to the consideration that it originated from an interpretative stance. Such will be its character in this paper.

Also, causality is here being postulated as solely physical, i.e., as physical states and processes. In connection with human behaviour, these states and processes will be seen as chiefly cerebro-neural. This must be borne in mind because I will, for reasons of linguistic and cultural convenience, be using mentalistic and psychologistic language in the course of arguing for determinism. In all cases, physical states and processes are what will be implied by the mentalistic terminology—even when I briefly mention, as part of the argument for determinism, cultural causation. My position, that all causes are physical, is one which, incidentally, accords with both physicalistic and epiphenomenalistic views of mind.

Given the above, let us consider the physical actions which can be seen as arising from physical causes. The Law of the Conservation of Energy asserts that every physical event/state is a carry-through of the energy informing the previous event/state. Permanent carry-through means no discontinuity, no absolutely new beginnings, hence no originality *ex nihilo*. Thus it is hard to conceive of a physical action that is not a derivate of a previous physical state or process.

The second argument for determinism is that, if there is no causal linkage between—on the one hand—motive, intention or decision to act and—on the other—the action itself, then the latter is irrational and chaotic in character. If it is free, it is not so in a rational or morally coherent way: that is, in the way required by those who ground their *moral* perspective in libertarianism, as do certain schools of religious thought.

In connection with this point, some libertarians focus attention on the fact that, in the physical sphere of brain processes, there is an element of pure randomness, through the uncaused activity of individual sub-atomic particles at the microscopic level. This arbitrariness is alleged to affect the course of large aggregates of atomic events at the macroscopic level: aggregates which would otherwise operate as causal factors. The randomness, by supposedly confounding causal process, is then said to create conditions for absolutely free action by the brain.

In reply, several points need to be made. One is to repeat that a freedom derived from total arbitrariness would have no rational character, would therefore lack moral coherence, and so could not legitimately be part of libertarian moral discourse. Another point is that, returning to purely physical considerations, no proof is available that randomness at the microscopic level does affect macroscopic processes in the brain. Moreover, given the manifest regularity of the brain's macroscopic operations as a result of evolutionary requirements for survival and successful adaptation, it is unlikely that randomness could have such an effect. If it did, brain processes (even allegedly *uncaused* ones) directed at survival, adaptation, and indeed all other purposes, would be continually thrown off course. This is not what happens.

Now, moving on from this point about brain processes: contrary to the claims of libertarians, the feeling of shame or remorse after committing what is deemed a bad action is not proof that the action was free in the sense of being uncaused. From the determinist standpoint, the feeling may be caused by the belief that the action was free. It may have other causes as well: temperament, acculturation.

Next, the feeling of extreme uncertainty, hesitancy and even anguished indecision before performing an action does not indicate that the action, when it eventually materialises, is uncaused. The hiatus, says determinism, is due to an enormously complicated and protracted interplay of factors and forces, an interplay which will finally issue in the triumph of a strongest factor, and the latter will then be the proximate cause of the action.

Further, despite its emphasis on causality, determinism does not eschew the concept of responsibility. A person is answerable for his actions in the sense of being the author of them and their consequences, and this responsibility can take a number of forms. If the person performed the action solely because he wanted and intended to, he is responsible for it in a voluntaristic sense. If he was forced to act by external coercive factors, without wanting to or voluntarily intending to, then his responsibility is non-voluntaristic. The same is the case if his action was accidental. It is chiefly voluntaristic responsibility which carries moral implications because it involves uncoerced intentions.

Responsibility of this kind does not preclude being blamed for the action, provided blame is based on moral appraisal of, firstly and mainly, intentions, and secondarily, consequences. In this section I will concentrate on intentions. Moral appraisal of intentions is itself justified because it is in accordance with general moral principles, which, if linked with determinism, affirm that intentions are *in themselves* unacceptable *even though they are effects*. Because such principles are general, they apply to every part of the causal sequence. They view each part in its own right, as being—in the moral sense but only in that sense—a discrete, self-contained entity. In this way, they *confer* moral quality on the entity in question. Thus, in declaring a certain intention to be—though caused—unacceptable, they confer on it the quality of unacceptability. The same reasoning applies, on the positive side, to intentions which, though also caused, are deemed to be commendable.

The defence of the above procedure may aptly be called the argument from conferred quality, and this is the argument I will regularly invoke from now on.

As a further point on general moral principles: it is quite appropriate to deploy them in the way described above. Criticism of behaviour is part of general moral discourse, whose basis must be concern for principles. It should be added that this concern is as legitimate a feature of moral perspectives which are inter-subjectivist and consensual as of those which claim to be objectivist. Inter-subjectivist ethics makes decisions, not alleged discoveries, regarding moral principles and what is intrinsically good or bad. Hence, it confers moral quality on things, in the way described previously.

The point about the legitimacy of principles in non-objectivist ethics needs to be emphasised. For atheistic determinism, which is my own position, the principles are caused by completely natural factors: biological and cultural. The primary factor is biological: the process of natural selection, which creates and extends a general capacity for moral responsiveness. The secondary factor is the growth of particular cultural formations; these are all facilitated by the general capacity, but channel it in various specific ways.

Hence the existence of any given set of moral principles is the outcome of a complex causal process; but, in line with my reasoning thus far, the principles are *not* on that account invalidated. If genuinely followed, they are the actual moral operatives in the society in which they obtain; and, where not challenged, must be acknowledged as such. Unless disputed, they must be respected as the effective moral agency. This is the case even though they have to be viewed in relative and contextual terms, as distinct from absolute and transcendental ones.

The above area of consideration now leads to the issue of the use of the word 'ought'. That use, because stemming from principles, is clearly context-dependent: a point which applies as much to our usage in contemporary Western culture as to that in other cultures. This must be borne in mind in relation to the material which now follows.

Any discussion of 'ought' inevitably leads to the issue of the relationship between 'ought' and 'can'. To tell a person that, as a matter of principle, he ought not to succumb to perverse impulses obviously only makes sense when that person possesses the capacity (itself caused) to respond to a moral appeal and to resist such impulses in the future. (There would be no point in making this appeal to, for example, a moral imbecile or a pathological recidivist.

The latter would have to be treated in a wholly restraining and preventative way, simply to preclude a repeat of the offending action.) Given, then, the capacity to perform the 'ought' in the future, the question that arises for determinists is the relation between 'ought' and 'can' in connection with past actions. Is it valid to invoke the argument from conferred quality/ moral principle with regard to past actions when, on determinism's own view, those actions were inextricably part of a causal sequence, and could therefore not have been other than they were? Is it valid, in other words, to say to a person: 'You ought not to have done X, even though, on that specific occasion, you could not have done other than X?'

The answer is: yes, it is valid, because the status of a moral principle as a basis for human well-being is unaffected by the miscellany of individual contexts. The morally capable person who, from whatever causes, has failed to live up to the principle, can comprehend his failure as fully as can other people. In this sense, he can understand why he ought not to have done what he was caused to do. Further, this understanding will hopefully be a causal factor activating his moral capacity in future behaviour.

Possession of moral capacity is a key consideration not only in relation to future conduct. While—to repeat—the determinist does not claim that the morally able person acted in an uncaused way in the past committal of wrongdoing, he does note that the person owns a moral potential which, for whatever reasons, was not activated on the occasion in question. Hence it is in the specific sense that this potential was not realised that the wrongdoer could not have acted otherwise. But if potential is realised in the future, from whatever causes, then future behaviour will be improved.

For determinism, improvement of future conduct is the central issue in ways of treating the malefactor. Such treatment, then, is reformative, not retributive. If past wrongdoing was caused, then treatment of a punitive nature is unjustified, no matter how strong a feeling of outrage and abhorrence the misdeed may understandably incur. There can be no philosophical legitimacy in punishing causality. (This point applies as much to wholly preventative action as to reformative.)

The above argument does not, of course, imply that reformative action will necessarily be mild. In fact, very tough action indeed may be deemed requisite to bring about the desired change in future motivation and conduct. But, no matter how austere, the treatment aims at producing constructive effects. The objective is to alter the malefactor's whole way of thinking and feeling, to instigate new causal sequences of intention and action—ones which are morally acceptable—and so to reform him from previous sequences which were unacceptable.

Also, the reform aimed at need not be of the 'change of heart' kind. The determinist is sufficiently realistic to know that some people's behaviour can be changed only by force of a deterrent; and instigating new causal sequences can be achieved as much by deterrence as by any other means. Deterrence is as much an effect as a change of heart, though, of course, a less congenial one.

The 'change of heart' argument applies even to someone sentenced to literal life imprisonment for murder. The sentence, while of course restraining and preventative, also aims, by its sheer severity, at producing an alteration in outlook, so that the murderer will be permanently appalled by homicidal impulses and will never again succumb to them. The result will hopefully be that he will try to lead a morally constructive life, even within the framework of life imprisonment.

Whereas the determinist can speak of different results in dealing with the wrongdoer, the libertarian is logically disqualified from doing so. He may speak, for example, of the 'aftermath of influences' or 'sequel to prior factors' but he clearly cannot avail himself of cause-and-effect vocabulary. Hence the question arises: why, for the libertarian, is firm and definite treatment of the wrongdoer considered appropriate? If such treatment will have, strictly speaking, no effect, why bother to apply it at all? The standard libertarian reply is that such treatment will 'incline without necessitating', and so leave intact the absolute freedom from which the person will subsequently act. However, if no treatment at all will also fail to necessitate, so essentially have the same sequel—again, why bother with treatment? If the point is repeated that the treatment will incline, three questions suggest themselves: first, what is the exact value of being inclined? Second, if it has any value, does that not lie in its being an effect of some kind, as the very wording, 'being inclined', implies? Third, if it is an effect, then why cannot the term be applied further, to do what the libertarian is committed to saying cannot be done: that is, to *explain*, as distinct from merely describing what happens after the inclining has taken place? It must be noted that libertarian discourse, without a causalist vocabulary, is confined to sequential description, indeed to mere narration.

In passing, it's worth noting that some critics of determinism argue that any tough treatment of wrongdoers is inappropriate on the grounds that, if their actions are caused, they are equivalent to accidental ones; and, for accidental actions which have harmful effects, harsh treatment is not usually applied. In reply, determinism avers that, when the causes of harmful actions are intentions and motives, these actions are *not* on a par with harmful ones which are purely accidental. The non-equivalence is due precisely to the presence of motives in connection with the former, and the absence of motives in connection with the latter. With the latter, there is manifestly no psychological situation requiring reform and improvement: no need for new motivation to replace old. By contrast, the intention-factor is the starting point for reformative action.

The critic of determinism might nevertheless attempt another version of the 'equivalence' argument by pointing out that, according to determinism, intentions are themselves caused, and so there is no justification in singling out one element in the causal process—the intentions—and choosing this as the basis for harsh treatment aimed at future improvement. If intentions are effects, then they are just as much part of a mechanistic concatenation as are all the factors involved in accidental actions. The determinist's reply begins with the repetition of the basic point that, yes, everything is part of a pervasive warp-and-woof of cause and effect. This includes, of course, the impulses to take action against wrongdoing and to engage in moral exhortation: impulses which, incidentally, do not lose their moral validity by being effects. The reply's next stage is to simply apply this point to the use of harsh treatment, and to reiterate what was said about the objective of instigating new, morally desirable, causal sequences. Here, the word 'objective' needs to be emphasised. There is no guarantee that the objective will be attained, since only omniscience could provide such a guarantee. But what the determinist is certain of is that the action taken in pursuit of the objective will have an effect of some kind: hopefully the one sought for, but perhaps another. In any event, the warp-and-woof of cause and effect will be, as always, in operation, and a strongest factor will triumph. The hope is to set up a sequence which will entail better intentions as both effects and as—crucially—causes, agencies.

Returning now to the previous point about reform: whereas the determinist can speak meaningfully about reforming the wrongdoer *from* something (i.e., a situation with a definite causal structure), the libertarian cannot. Libertarians, believing in absolute free-will, regard this freedom as an unalterable reality. Also, many libertarians see this freedom as not only unchangeable but also, in value-terms, as good, because providing a basis for moral judgement. If, then, the context is that of free actions which are morally unacceptable and need to be changed, what exactly is the malefactor to be reformed from? Not from his absolute freedom, since that is allegedly unchangeable; nor from that freedom if it is a good. From what, then? The difficulty in answering these questions reinforces the determinist argument that it is only in a causalist discourse that the concept of reform can be fruitfully employed.

The causalist perspective covers not only the moral capacity previously discussed, but all capacity. If it is accepted that pre-natal genetic processes lay the foundations for all capacities, and therefore create a genotype which post-natal environment then moulds into a specific phenotype, it must also be accepted that, for each individual, ability is finite. The genotype is formed by processes which are of one kind and not another; therefore these processes can only have one outcome and not another. Process A is not process B or C, and so on, and the same applies to its upshot. Clearly, only a genetic process consisting of components without limit could produce capacity without limit. Finite ability to act means a finite sphere of possible action. That sphere, then, is a conditioned one.

It perhaps needs to be added that, in any given environment, the emergent phenotype is not necessarily the only one that could have been derived from the genotype. Other phenotypes were perhaps possible (though, if so, ones with similarities to each other). However, the main point is that the number of possible phenotypes is limited, as indeed it must be, given the finite character of genotype formation.

I'd now like to say something more about the concept of relative freedom I referred to in the introduction, and to outline the kind of vocabulary I regard as most appropriate to determinist discourse. In doing so, I will echo a number of things already said.

The concept of relative freedom is, as most of you will have probably anticipated, that of compatibilism. Compatibilism, as you know, does contain a notion of free-will, but one very different from that held by libertarians. Whereas libertarians speak of total and unconditioned freedom of action, compatibilists have a more modest and limited position: an action is free when it is not the result of external coercion or force. It is free, therefore, if the unhindered *result* of volitions *within* the individual: the unimpeded expression of what the individual wishes to do. As such, it is the effect of internal causes, but of these alone. In this sense, free-will is compatible with causation. Hence compatibilism is deterministic. It is the only framework within which determinism employs the concept of free-will. (It's worth noting, in passing, that several distinguished philosophers who have been determinists have been compatibilists: examples include Spinoza, Hobbes, Leibniz and Locke.)

A further point about compatibilism is that freedom to do what one wishes does not, as Schopenhauer says, imply freedom to choose what one wishes. Wishes, desires and aspirations are unchosen *givens*, to be acted on or otherwise, but not things the individual has selected or adopted. They result from, again, phenotype formation: an interactive process between environment and factors which are largely hereditary: a process of which the individual, in his earliest formative years, is the done-to, not the doer. The process is a matter of potential, genetic in derivation, being activated by whatever stimuli its environment provides; and it is as a product of this process that the individual wishes, desires and aspires. Once again, we see determinism at work.

Also, despite the pre-environmental possibility of more than one phenotype being formed, the one that actually does materialise turns out to be remarkable in its consistency. If we designate the formed phenotype in psychological terms as 'temperament', 'character' or 'personality', then we know, from direct experience of ourselves and others, the continuity this involves. Not for nothing did the ancient Greeks derive their word for 'character' from their word for 'custom'. In fact, individuals are knowable, both to themselves and others, only by virtue of this continuity. In no other way could persons be stable objects of knowledge, as distinct from formless fluxes, chaoses devoid of definable identity and structure. In no other way, therefore, could they be predictable, which we indeed regard them as being when we are sure we know them well. For no other reason do we with confidence assign epithets to them such as 'honest', 'reliable' or 'conscientious'—and to apply to their future behaviour as well as to their present and past. Within no other framework could fictional characters in great literature register on us as intelligible and true to life. On no other basis, finally, does the famous Delphic injunction 'Know thyself' makes sense to us. Such consistency, the determinist argues, is the product of repeated causal sequences.

Returning to the freedom to act, as defined by compatibilism, there is a case for using vocabulary of an activist and dynamic kind in describing caused actions which have a highly positive moral character. While such actions can be validly designated as 'effects', 'results' or 'consequences', these words are arguably incomplete descriptors, because passivist. They fail to convey the energic quality indicated above. Let's think of verbs which are used to denote morally momentous actions: verbs such as 'inspire', 'move', 'stimulate', 'challenge'. The actions which result from being inspired, moved, stimulated and challenged can be dynamic to the highest degree, with their own splendour and dignity. Also, they can have rich and productive consequences. Hence they merit a wider range of diction than passivist vocabulary provides. Terms such as 'deed', 'act of courage,' 'gesture of justified defiance' and 'brave attempt' all contain the activist quality that is needed here. An action requires, after all, action-words for its adequate description.

Such language applies, of course, not only to actions but also to the whole selfhood from which actions emanate. From the compatibilist standpoint, the self, though an effect, is an agency, a force, a flow, a pushing in a certain direction. Thus the active, expressive self 'selves', to use a verb coined by the poet Gerard Manley Hopkins.

A further area of linguistic consideration is to do with the diction of praise and blame. It has previously been contended, in relation to the argument from conferred quality and moral principle, that caused actions can be justifiably praised or blamed. Nevertheless, the perspective in which plaudit or castigation is expressed obviously differs from that of libertarianism. This difference needs to be emphasised, as part of the critique of libertarianism.

Libertarian notions of praise and blame are in fact the traditional ones, found in most cultures past and present, and based on the view that, if human action is always subject to causation, then the language of plaudit and censure is robbed of most, if not all, its meaning. According to this view, the use of such language reflects the universal recognition of the reality of absolute free-will; and to abandon this recognition and the linguistic usage that goes with it would be to undermine the central feature of people's moral dealings with each other, and to cause massive cultural upheaval. (A notable advocate of this position was Sir Isaiah Berlin.)

Leaving aside the argument from custom and tradition which this position contains, I wish to propose that the libertarian use of praise and blame language reflects not only the belief in absolute freedom but also, and more importantly, psychological factors: deeply ingrained, and understandable, ways of responding to actions regarded as moral or immoral. What is present in these responses is an acute, immediate and dramatic consciousness of the action's intentions and consequences. This consciousness produces praise if the action had benevolent intentions and beneficial consequences; and blame if the intentions and consequences were harmful. There are also, incidentally, cases where an action with benevolent intentions misfires, and for this reason produces blame.

The above ways of thinking and feeling fail to consider causes of intentions, and causal linkage between intention and action (hence, of course, the belief in absolute free-will). Also, this omission explains why, sometimes, an obviously unintended and wholly accidental action that leads to harmful consequences becomes an object of blame. In all cases, what is happening is a concentration, in the form of approval or disapproval, on certain features of the action-context, but not on all.

For the determinist, by contrast, there is an all-inclusive consideration of the action-context, one that involves full regard for causality and so transcends the psychological limitations outlined above. At the same time, this regard does not exclude appraisal language. In addition to what has been said about the argument from conferred quality and moral principle, points can be made about an appraisal language which, unlike the traditional and predominant kind, is adequately attuned to causality.

This language, in the case of praiseworthy action, focuses equally on intention and consequence, regarding each as both effect and beneficial factor. It does not withhold praise on grounds that the good intention was the result of prior factors: it places the same value on the conferred quality of the intention as it does on the action proceeding from the intention.

In the case of blameworthy action, diction focuses on action and consequences. While viewing bad intentions as being as much an effect as good ones, it obviously finds nothing worthy in the former, and saves comment for the bad action and its results. Where the wrongdoer is morally capable, it says, in effect: 'While your intention and action were caused, just look at the awful consequences of what you have done. Given those consequences, resolve never to repeat the action.' Thus, blame-diction appeals to the malefactor's conscience, to his capacity for appreciating the suffering he has brought to others, and to his potential for self-improvement.

In the above ways, a deterministic language of plaudit and censure could, if universally adopted, become a new centre-point for our moral dealings with each other, replacing a traditional linguistic mode which has manifestly failed to cognise fully the actual facts of behaviour.

Finally, I'd like to enlarge on a point which was previously given only incidental status. You'll recall that I said earlier that the impulses to take action against wrongdoing and to engage in moral exhortation do not lose their ethical validity by being effects. This point, though implicit in much of this paper, needs to be emphasised. Firstly, it shows the role that prescriptive and evaluative elements play in a discourse which is otherwise descriptive and explanatory. Determinism, while it always takes care to specify the causes of moral actions, always values those actions. To explain, then, is not to de-value.

Secondly, and directly following on from the previous sentence, consider the case of a man of kindly and sensitive disposition who is standing by a river and sees a child fall in. The child cannot swim. The man feels an urge to save the child, dives in and effects a rescue. Both the libertarian and determinist would praise the action, but from crucially different angles. For the libertarian, the action is laudable because it is *not* an effect, not a result of the urge previously referred to. It is admirable because it is causeless. By contrast, it is admirable to the determinist partly *because of* its causal connection to the urge; the latter in turn is laudable because it is an emanation from a humane temperament. The action has been explicated; but this should not reduce the plaudits by a single one.

An Inclusive Moral Theory

Like any outlook which claims to encompass every aspect of reality, both ontologically and ethically, secularism requires an inclusive moral theory: a theory which embraces the full spectrum of human vitality, aspiration, responsiveness, inter-action. Such a theory is to be found in the position which seeks to maximise harmony between impulses (and here is meant only impulses, not actions arising from them).

The principle of compatibility is essentially secularist in that the object of moral appraisal is not individual impulses themselves but their relation to each other. The relational view lies at the heart of secularism because it involves acceptance of neo-Darwinism, and therefore of the view that individual impulses, because products of capacities generated by the non-moral process which evolution has been, are not—in isolation—subject to moral judgement.[1] These impulses have the same non-moral character as their ultimate source, which has been a purposeless biological sequence. What should be judged, then, is the co-ordination of impulses; only at this collective or *ensemble* level does morality become an issue.

Such is the case because the attempt to harmonise impulses is an act of both individual and group significance, concerned with achieving equilibrium both within the individual and between him and the collective; in fact, the individual's internal balance is a pre-requisite for a balanced relation with the group. Hence the act is of a social and moral nature. It is to be distinguished from the individual's act of merely recognising within himself a variety of impulses, as existential data, and comprehending these as, to repeat, the non-moral resultant of the non-moral evolutionary process. That act is only cognitive, not ethical: only a perception of what the materials are on which he has to do moral work. In other words, the individual has to move from a purely scientific stance, in which impulses are seen as effects of causes, as—so to speak—a neutral power-pool, to a

[1] For decisive arguments that the evolutionary processes leading up to man possessed no moral character or significance whatsoever, see especially the writings of Anthony Flew.

stance in which decisions must be made on how that power is to be directed.

Here, the difference between secular and (most) religious ethics should be noted. Most religious systems categorise individual impulses as good or bad; in other words, they apply moral judgements independently of relational considerations. Thus their approach is absolute rather than relative. Such absolutism derives chiefly from two sources: firstly, moral cognitivism, the claim to possess knowledge of what is good and bad, a knowledge allegedly derived from deity; secondly, and relatedly, insufficient knowledge of the evolutionary basis of impulses.

It may be objected, in defence of the absolutist approach, that, for example, the impulse to kill someone because he has done nothing more than insult you is, in and by itself, evil; and does *not become* evil by being considered in the light of very different impulses, e.g., to sympathise with, help, be unselfish. However, the question must be asked: on what precise basis is the impulse regarded as absolutely and intrinsically bad? The only basis would appear to be moral cognitivism; but this position entails enormous difficulties from a scientific standpoint, and is, in any case, one which few if any secularists now adhere to. If, then, a non-cognitivist approach is adopted, the argument becomes a relativist one: that the murderous impulse is incompatible with humane impulses, ones which any normally constituted person will both possess and value; hence that it must be rejected on grounds of incompatibility.

Further, and pivotally, this rejection is not of a logical kind; it is not like rejecting a mathematical proposition because it clashes with the established canons of mathematics. For the non-cognitivist and relativist, the principle of compatibility is rooted not in logic but in feeling, and stems from a felt need to create cohesion between different emotional positions. Logic, by contrast, has no cohesive role in ethics. In fact, it has no primary or fundamental role at all. It is neither the factor causing impulses, nor constituting them, nor seeking to harmonise them. The latter two factors are exclusively affective; and the harmonising factor is an emotional urge to maximise the satisfaction of all other emotions: because, the greater the compatibility between feelings, the greater the satisfaction gained from each of them.

Thus, an impulse whose satisfaction will be at the expense of the satisfaction of other impulses is likely, in any person of foresight, to be rejected in favour of the latter. In terms of emotional interests, there is a kind of democratic—indeed, utilitarian— system at work:

the minority must not harm the majority, and well-being is to be maximised.

The foundational status of feeling in the psychic situation described above clearly indicates that, in secular ethical systems, rationality (including logic) is part of the superstructure, not the base, because it is concerned with devising means by which the satisfaction of impulses, desires and aspirations – that is, ends – may be attained. Reason would only be foundational if, firstly, moral knowledge of right and wrong existed, and was acquirable by the intellect; or secondly, if impulses, and the drive[2] to co-ordinate them, were the product of ratiocination. On the view that neither is the case, reason can be defined as having a secondary and instrumental role, one which determines means, rather than a primary one which determines ends.

This view of the place of rationality in ethics is of course Humean, and echoes Hume's famous dictum that reason is, and always should be, the 'slave of the passions'. The fact that emotion is the bedrock of ethics serves to remind us of the dangers of the naturalistic fallacy: the fallacy of attempting to derive a moral 'ought' from a factual 'is'. Again, Hume can be invoked, specifically his view that it is 'altogether inconceivable' how 'ought' statements can be deduced from 'is' ones.[a] The affective basis of morality, invalidating as it does all claim to objective knowledge of good and bad, means that ethical discourse, unlike scientific, focuses not on the ascertaining of facts but on the ascertaining and discussing of *attitudes* to facts. Attitudes are feeling-positions; and they constitute moral values. Also, taking sides in ethical discourse means defending or attacking attitudes and values – arguing for or against them. This must inevitably be the case because, to repeat, the focus is not on fact and knowledge. At all times in this discourse, the naturalistic fallacy must be studiously avoided; for, just as it is fallacious to argue from a fact about the natural world to an endorsement of that fact, so it is unacceptable to contend that the fact of possessing an attitude or value is itself a justification for possessing it. Once again, attitudes have to be argued for, extensively and painstakingly. Further, the ultimate aim of such argumentation is to appeal to the feelings of the listener.

The natural extension of this point is that advocacy of an inclusive moral theory, based on the idea of maximal affective satisfaction for

---

[2] Some people might want to describe this drive as 'rational' simply because it seeks co-ordination; but, given what has been said about the nature of the drive, this term is unhelpful.

the normally constituted, non-pathological individual, is a project ultimately seeking to produce an emotional effect in those to whom it is directed. No other objective can or should be claimed for it.

The secularist's view is that such a theory effectively replaces the moral perspective offered by religion. The secularist acknowledges the very important ethical role played by religion in the course of human development—indeed, he regards this function[3] as by far religion's chief contribution to that development; but he also regards it as now superseded by secular morality. The latter commands much fuller understanding of the affective mainsprings of moral experience than could ever have possibly been possessed by the religious mentality, which was pre-Darwinian and which saw—still sees—the source of moral principles as lying outside mankind.

Emotional inclusiveness and equilibrium as a moral ideal have been advocated by various philosophers since ancient times, most notably Plato and Aristotle. Their most prominent secular spokesman in the twentieth century has perhaps been Santayana. Timothy Sprigge, in his illuminating study of Santayana, speaks of the emphasis placed by the philosopher on 'the impulse to organise other impulses, or the interest in organising other interests ... into a harmonious system.' Hence for Santayana the truly moral man is the one 'who has as his controlling ideal a form of life in which a maximum of impulses find a harmonious satisfaction.'[b] Such a man 'preserves at each moment a sense of the value of all that he ever values, and lives by an ideal which, so far as it is possible, synthesises them all, making none the sole arbiter of the remainder's right ...'[c]

Another important twentieth-century proponent of this ideal was I. A. Richards. Interestingly, Richards was not primarily a philosopher but a literary critic. He formulated what he called a 'Psychological Theory of Value', on the basis of which he argued that the conduct of life is 'throughout an attempt to organise impulses so that success is obtained for the greater number or mass of them, for the most important and the weightiest set.'[d] Accordingly for Richards, any impulse is valid if it does not involve the frustration of an equal or more important one. Morality, then, is a matter of appropriate organisation of impulses. Also, it is worth noting that Richards, as literary critic, regards literature—at least good literature—as being valuable partly because it offers outstanding examples of such

---

[3] For definitive secular commentary on this role, see in particular Santayana's *Reason in Religion*, Durkheim's *Les formes elementaires de la vie religieuse*, and Feuerbach's *The Essence of Christianity*.

organisation. (Here, incidentally, he echoes E. M. Forster and his dictum 'Only connect'.)

The outlooks of Santayana and Richards (among others) constitute the all-embracing moral approach pertinent to the neo-Darwinian perspective with which almost all secularists concur. They are modern versions of eudaemonism (the happiness-principle), appropriate to a culture which is either atheistic or agnostic. No constructive satisfaction, nor any form of intelligent edification which religion once supplied, lies outside their parameters; and within those parameters, great action and great art reside.

Endnotes

[a] In the *Treatise of Human Nature* (1740), book 3, section 1.

[b] Timothy Sprigge, *Santayana* (1974), (London and New York: Routledge, 1995) p. 198, for both quotations.

[c] *Ibid.*, p. 202.

[d] As quoted by Raymond Williams in *Culture and Society, 1780-1950*, Penguin Books edn., 1977 (1958), p. 241.

Human Necessities and Human Liberties

> What is peculiar and novel to our age is that the principal goal of politics in every advanced society is not, strictly speaking, a political one; that is to say, it is not concerned with human beings as persons and citizens, but with human bodies, with the precultural, prepolitical human creature ... the main political issue today is concerned not with human liberties but with human necessities.[a]
>
> W. H. Auden

Let us examine what Auden is saying. Firstly, he argues that to view a human being in a fully-fledged political sense is to see him as a person and citizen, i.e., as a distinct individual with a distinct life-style, someone with highly specific political and cultural orientations. This is the politics concerned with 'human liberties'. Auden adds that modern politics is in fact not concerned with this kind of specificity, but with more general and elementary issues: meeting basic needs—which, by implication, means such things as providing material security, ensuring physical well-being, and supplying basic education. This, of course, is the politics of 'human necessities'.

How far Auden is actually correct in this characterisation of contemporary politics in advanced societies is open to question and will be discussed later; but, apart from that, his words serve an important purpose in distinguishing between two kinds of political approach. This distinction should always be borne in mind, especially by those who advocate political programmes. Advocates should always be clear whether their objectives are geared toward the supplying of necessities or of liberties—or of both.

It is arguable that the meeting of necessities is a means to the end of creating opportunity for the enjoyment of liberties. Certainly the former is a precondition for the latter: self-development, cultural exploration, complex choosing and the drawing of fine distinctions are all obviously impossible without first being physically safe, adequately fed and sheltered, and sufficiently educated.

Having said this, though, we should add that in the modern world the distinction between necessities and liberties is not as clear-cut as it might first appear. Many of the things we might readily categorise as 'necessities' have, since World War II and the UN Declaration of Human Rights, come under the heading of 'freedoms', e.g., freedom from hunger, persecution, violence. The closeness in meaning between the words 'freedom' and 'liberty' indicates the semantic difficulty involved. However, perhaps a way out of this complexity is to use the word 'liberty' only in connection with the idea of performing actions—voluntarily and without coercion—to achieve satisfaction of some kind. Hence we would not speak of 'liberty from' as we do of 'freedom from', but only of 'liberty to'. Employing the word in this way, we can return to the distinction drawn by Auden and again appreciate its usefulness.

Also in returning to Auden, we can contend that his argument about the prevalence of 'necessity politics', while dubious when applied to the advanced societies of the Western world, is generally sound when applied to the societies of the Third World. In the latter, problems of poverty and scarcity are so extensive as to be—unsurprisingly— the main issues on the political agenda of the majority who suffer from them. (It might be added that these problems afflicted the majority of the population in most Western societies until some way into the twentieth century, though in a generally less severe form.) The reasons for these problems are manifold, and have a great deal to do with unfair trade policies pursued by the world's wealthiest nations.[1]

These considerations give rise to the question: is it fair to ask that a 'liberty politics' be pursued in Third World countries in addition to a 'necessity politics'? In other words, is it reasonable to expect Third World populations, given the severe pressures they are under, to be just as concerned with such things as cultural exploration as they are with securing food, clean water and literacy?

This is not an easy question to answer. It might be contended that it is completely unreasonable to expect a politics of liberty: that progressive forces in the Third World should, at present, focus exclusively on meeting the basic needs of their peoples, given the colossal dimensions of those needs. The argument has much cogency. However, it could also entail problems: because what it could lead to is a concentration on elementary issues so intense that complex

[1] These policies include: forcing Third World producers of primary commodities to accept insultingly low prices for their produce; imposing high tariffs on imports of manufactured goods from Third World countries; and flooding these countries with Western agricultural produce which can be sold at very cheap prices because the production was subsidised—so depriving indigenous produce of a market outlet.

issues—those to do with a politics of liberty—come to be seen as unimportant and unworthy of consideration. In other words, a politics of necessity could become an end in itself, as distinct from a means or conduit to another kind of politics. This attitude could congeal into an authoritarian paternalism, according to which the body politic declares itself to know the full extent of what is best for society. Such paternalism has, in the past, been evident in the history of Communist states, principally the Soviet Union and China, and its dire cultural (and political) consequences have been clear to see.

Perhaps the best way to answer the question is to grant a politics of necessity the centre-stage position for the present, but to insist that this position be provisional only—that, in due course, a politics of liberty should make its entry and grow in importance, perhaps eventually becoming central. This insistence would only be fair to Third World society. If the concern is genuinely to create/increase happiness, the obvious acknowledgement must be made that happiness does not come from the satisfaction of basic needs alone: a psychological fact to which human history has repeatedly attested. In varying degree, people need to be inspired, uplifted, taken out of the banality of daily routine. These experiences come from the exploration of liberty, from cultural and moral engagement of a distinctive kind (and one which, ideally, should be free of false views of reality).

If, now, we leave the Third World context and look at the advanced societies of the West, we can again go back to Auden's words, and add to our previous commentary on them by saying that Western politics is an interesting mixture of 'necessity' and 'liberty' elements, with neither element predominant. Emphasis on meeting necessities is to be found on the Left, its traditional locus. Concern with furthering liberties exists to some extent on the Left, but much more so in the Liberal-Centre. (The Right is chiefly concerned with either preserving or extending the power of big business, so has no place in this discussion.)

To a considerable extent, the concerns with necessity and liberty converge around the issue of equality of opportunity. Everyone on the Left advocates this equality, arguing that it is a basic right and need. (The Leftist argument also, of course, includes the contention that such equality is impossible while society remains socially and economically divided in the way it is under capitalism.) In this advocacy, the Left is at one with the Liberal-Centre, which fully upholds the principle of an equal chance for all. However, there remains a difference in emphasis. Centrists see equal opportunity mainly as a means for developing individuality and the enjoyment of liberties both economic and cultural, whereas many on the Left regard it as an end in itself: a 'marker', so to speak, that class privilege has been overcome.

Criticisms of both attitudes can be made. Many Centrists, while justifiably interested in the development of individual capacity and variety, can be faulted for lacking a counter-balancing sense of overall social cohesion and unity. Many Leftists, on the other hand, can be censured for failing to examine the full implication of equality of opportunity. While the full attainment of such equality would undoubtedly be an historic social achievement, what it would do would be to maximise the display of capacity-differences between individuals, and so open the way to new kinds of differentiation within society: not differences based on class power and privilege, no, but differences all the same. These would be totally meritocratic. As a related point, a good deal of this differentiation would be hierarchical in an occupational and professional sense. In other words, equality of opportunity would lead to inequality, i.e., superiority and inferiority, in performance and so in status. Indeed, the principle of equality of opportunity would be meaningless if it did not imply such consequences; there would clearly be no sense in speaking of equality of opportunity to be undifferentiated from everybody else. Hence the principle is egalitarian only up to a point; this is what many on the Left overlook.[2]

The shortcomings in the outlooks of many on the Left and in the Liberal-Centre can be summed up by saying that both viewpoints, because of their respective emphases, lack a sufficient sense of society as a kind of unity in diversity. Many Leftists need to be reminded that unity should not mean uniformity, and many Centrists that diversity should not mean atomisation. An adequate vision of social cohesion can only come from a full appreciation of the values contained in the politics of both necessity and liberty.

---

[2] In general connection with these points, see Santayana: 'Social democracy at high pressure would leave no room for liberty. The only free man in it would be the one whose whole ideal was to be an average man.' See *The Wisdom of Santayana*, p. 35.

Endnote

[a] W.H. Auden, *The Dyer's Hand and Other Essays* (London: Faber and Faber, 1963) p. 87.

Reflections on the Resurgence of the Left

This text is reproduced by kind permission of the editor of the journal *The Ethical Record*.

This resurgence, in Western Europe and North America, dates from the late 1990s. It comes as the culmination of a gathering mood of protest against the view, promulgated since the 1980s, that there is no alternative to monopoly capitalism, and to economic globalisation under the aegis of the monopoly system. That view was strongly promoted in the 1980s by Reaganism and Thatcherism, and has not been questioned by subsequent Western governments. It sought reinforcement at the end of the 1980s in the collapse of the Soviet Union and the latter's satellite regimes in Eastern Europe; and it found reinforcement in the actual increase in power which multinational corporations (MNCs) enjoyed during the 80s and 90s. The reaction against it, after a long period in which many on the Left had felt disheartened by the seemingly inexorable strengthening of international capitalism and its so-called 'neo-liberal' agenda, marks a new lease of life for the anti-capitalist movement, a new spirit of purpose, tenacity and, most important, co-operation: there is now more national and international co-ordination on the Left than there has been for a generation. Evidence of this is to be found, for example, in England, with the recent formation of the Socialist Alliance, and, at the international level, in the creation of the European and World Social Forums.

It is noteworthy that this resurgence has come at a time when the United States, the world's only remaining super-power, has displayed increasing arrogance, and contempt for international law and opinion, in its foreign policy. The current period is not, of course, the only one in which such arrogance has been shown: US intervention in Vietnam and other parts of Indo-China in the 1960s and 70s is a previous example. However, the chief difference between earlier instances of aggressive foreign policy and current ones is that now there is little attempt at justification in terms of universal values such as 'defence of freedom/democracy/human rights'. The language is now much more overtly nationalistic and power-referenced.[1] The US openly declares that it is primarily concerned with its 'national interest', an interest succinctly defined in 1999 by William Cohen, Defense Secretary in the Clinton administration, as bound up with 'ensuring uninhibited access to key markets, energy supplies and strategic resources' around the world.[a] Indeed, under the current Bush administration, the wording has become even more extreme, with the avowal that the US now seeks 'full spectrum dominance' in world affairs.

Returning to Cohen's phrasing: his blunt admission that the national interest is about exerting global economic control is seen by the Left as an accurate definition. The Left generally regards these economic goals as principally those of the American MNCs, whose influence on government is enormous. Also, the Left's general view is that, among these MNCs, the oil and energy industries have paramount influence with the current Bush administration.

This position has a great deal of cogency. Nevertheless, some on the Left take the view that the political power-structure in the US (covering not just the Bush presidency but also other recent ones) reflects the interests not only of American monopoly capital but of monopolies world-wide. They argue that a transnational monopolisitc elite, originating from a variety of countries, has arisen, and seeks representation by the world's most powerful political structure—the Washington establishment. While it is true that a large section of this elite is American, the key consideration, according to this argument, is that the elite *as a whole* seeks to work in unison, through strategic alliances, cartels and mergers; as a whole, therefore, it seeks a political arm. Hence, this argument concludes, national capitalist interest really means transnational capitalist interest.[b]

A third view is in conflict with this position, and is a variant on the first: that, while American capitalism seeks global domination, so other national capitalisms wish to prevent that hegemony, and to

---

[1] Such language has in fact been used in the past as well, sporadically but significantly. One of the most telling instances was as long ago as 1948, when the State Department averred: 'We need not deceive ourselves that we can afford the luxury of altruism and world benefaction ... we should cease to talk about ... unreal objectives such as human rights, the raising of living standards and democratisation. The day is not far off when we are going to have to deal in *straight power concepts* [italics mine].' (As quoted by Mark Curtis, in *The Ambiguities of Power: British Foreign Policy since 1945*, Zed Books Ltd., London and New Jersey, 1995, pp. 17–18.)

secure for themselves a significant share of the world's resources, particularly oil. It is in these terms that many on the Left interpret the recent rift between, on the one hand, the US, and, on the other, France, Germany and Russia, over American intentions to invade Iraq: European capitalism did not want to see the US gain sole control over Iraqi oil.

Whatever the precise reality of the situation, the Left is undoubtedly correct in asserting what is common to all three viewpoints: that MNC influence on Western governments is the chief political and economic danger in the contemporary world.

In considering ways to combat this danger, many on the Left resort to the traditional Marxist argument that the solution lies with the 'working class'. This term is, in practice, usually employed to mean, not everybody who sells his/her labour power in the job market, but the majority of those who do: in other words, those not of high-level occupational status. This kind of class perspective is based on the postulate that it is the majority of workers who are exploited the most under the capitalist system, while being the ones who actually produce the wealth by which the system thrives.

On this argument, a number of comments can be made. Firstly, in most Western societies, it is true that lower-status workers are, on the whole, paid less than those higher up the professional ladder. However, this is as true of employees working in public services as in the private industrial/commercial sectors. So, income differences are not just a feature of capitalism; while these differences are indeed wider in the capitalist sphere than in any other, they are not confined to it, and therefore cannot always be ascribed to economic exploitation. This point leads to the question of whether, in any complex society with a division of labour based on differing levels of ability, responsibility and training, there will always be some measure of income variation grounded on these differences. Even in a complex society without economic exploitation, such differences would be present; and so too, probably, would be the demand for variations in pay. Hence, while the Left are justified in protesting against income discrepancies based on exploitation, they are unrealistic—and even, arguably, unjust—if they extend that protest to opposition to the *principle* of income differentiation. Unfortunately, some on the Left do make that extension.

Secondly, again in most Western societies, many lower-status workers are not actually engaged in producing wealth, in the traditional sense of manufacturing consumer goods. In addition to those working in public services, there are many others employed, for example, in commerce, banking, and service industries. Hence, extensive modification has to be made to the afore-mentioned concept of the 'working class'. As has been implied, a wide range of socio-economic descriptions can be applied to lower-status workers, and this range is not fully encompassed by the term 'working class' as traditionally used by the Left.

A further problem with the traditional use of the term is the embedded assumption that the lower-status workers constituting the 'class' are a homogenous group, evincing little variation in intellectual and cultural orientation, not to mention moral drive. This assumption is a central difficulty: it prevents many on the Left from recognising that these workers, taken individually, are an extremely mixed group, as indeed is every large social group. Failure to discern this variability and complexity can produce two results: (1) The individuality of specific members of the 'class' may be under- estimated, so that individuals are defined too rigidly in class terms. (2) The moral and intellectual shortcomings of many members may go unnoticed.

On result (2), it should be immediately added that these shortcomings are obviously not confined to lower-status workers. This, in fact, is part of a larger social point that needs to be made: that moral and intellectual weakness is a problem at all social levels of present-day society (as of past societies), and will not be abolished by sociological oversimplifications.

In the contemporary world, we see clear disparities in people's intellectual, cultural and moral achievements, as much among lower-status workers as between them and other groups. Questions for the Left are these: would such differences exist even in a society without economic exploitation? Or, in such a society, would we find the parity in cultural and moral performance which is so conspicuously absent now? Again in contemporary society, we see personal rivalry, love of power, and egotism of various kinds. Would these disappear with the end of economic exploitation, or would they instead take—as they often do now—a variety of non-economic forms?

Finally, again in connection with intellectual activity, many people in modern society find it difficult to meet the rigorous demands of a scrupulously scientific and rationalistic culture. Barring the restoration of religion to its nineteenth-century status, these demands will persist and even multiply. Will many people, 'working class' and otherwise, continue to have difficulty with them, even in an exploitation-free context; and will they therefore (as often happens now) take the line of least resistance and revert to religious belief or other anti-scientific ways of thinking?

Many more questions could be asked, but the ones posed here, plus the points which preceded them, are sufficient to indicate the problems surrounding the concept of the 'working class' that is still widely held on the Left. Given these problems, we return to the question of how to combat the danger posed by MNC influence on governments. The strategy I wish to advocate involves a radical enlargement of the concept we have been discussing. In the light of what has been said about the hazards presented by monopoly capitalism, I propose that 'working class' should now invariably mean: anyone who works for a living, in the sense of earning a wage or salary, and who does not support the monopoly system by either working in or for it, or by investing in it, or by engaging in financial speculation connected with it. The term might even be extended to owners of small businesses who wish to confine themselves to small-scale enterprise, and who also do not support the monopoly system. Thus the term becomes applicable to a huge variety of occupations, professions and income-levels.

Such variety is a crucial factor; and expanding the meaning of the term 'working class' has a number of very important consequences. Firstly, the attack on the monopoly system now carries a moral appeal which is socially inclusive, in contrast to the exclusiveness of the Left's standard class concept. No longer is the moral call solely to lower-status workers, as if the latter were collectively the salt of the earth. Secondly, as a related point, the capacities of exceptionally able people can be enlisted. Many individuals of high professional status possess extraordinary capacities, and these will be gold-dust in both the effort to dismantle the monopoly system and to establish and administer a non-exploitative one. Thirdly, variety constitutes a truly popular front: the full social and cultural spectrum is represented; the popular movement is seen as consisting of *individuals,* all distinctive, many from different walks of life, but all sharing a common purpose.

Already, in fact, the movement against global capital is displaying considerable social variety. For example, the abundance of teachers, lecturers, lawyers, journalists and media workers in its ranks is ample evidence of the need to revise and expand traditional notions of the 'working class'. Variegation and diversity were on display at gatherings of the European and World Social Forums in 2002. This was also the case on the two-million strong march in London in February 2003 against US plans to invade Iraq, and on other anti-war marches in other capitals; and it is to be hoped that most of the anti-war protesters will join the anti-globalisation movement.

As an overall point, the social breadth manifest in the opposition to monopoly capitalism should be increased, and there is no reason why, given effective dissemination of information about MNCs, this cannot happen relatively easily. We would then have a global civil society movement pitted against the oligarchy of corporate power. The majority of people in Western society, as in the world as a whole, have no stake in monopoly capitalism: they are not involved in running it, are not major shareholders in it (or shareholders at all), and do not engage in financial speculation in connection with it. Even allowing for a sizeable measure of political apathy and general petty-mindedness among the majority, that still leaves a very large number of potential supporters, far larger than the number supporting the monopoly system. While it is true that the degree of commitment displayed by these potential supporters would vary, nevertheless the sum total of commitment would be considerable.

The need for, and fact of, diversity in the current struggle against capitalist globalisation should be seen against the background of the historical reality that many, perhaps most, radical movements have consisted of combinations of social groups, not just one group. Major examples include the English and French revolutions against monarchical power, in the seventeenth and eighteenth centuries respectively; the European revolutions of 1848; and English Chartism in the early nineteenth century. In these and other cases, there has been an inter-group recognition of the injustice of the status quo.

Further, a highly developed sense of social variety means that, in the effort to achieve reform, meritocratic values are not overlooked. If a society free of economic exploitation is to be a genuinely open society, diversity of earned status and reputation will be one of its key features. Differentiation and justifiable hierarchy (as distinct, of course, from the unjustifiable kind) will be among its hallmarks. It has already been said that some people on the Left are not sufficiently mindful of meritocratic considerations. They seem to think that a non-exploitative society will be automatically one without rank, degree or gradation of any kind. In particular, they do not see that even a collective economic system will require key positions, and therefore people of exceptional ability to occupy them effectively. Such a view results from failure, as previously noted, to understand the full implications of equality of opportunity; it is to be hoped that this failure will not persist.

'Another world is possible' is one of the leading slogans of the movement against monopoly capital. The slogan is certainly accurate, but what must always be remembered is that this alternative society, if fully meritocratic, will be highly complex. This complexity will engender moral and cultural difficulties, especially with regard to the relationship between those who are highly scrupulous in the moral and intellectual senses, and those who are not; and between those who are highly original and creative, and those who are not. These difficulties are already sufficiently evident in present-day society, and there is no reason to think they will simply disappear as a result of economic changes. Moreover, such problems will be additional to the constant challenge of ensuring that society remains non-exploitative in the economic and political senses. In brief, the other world for which all progressive people strive will not be unproblematic.

Endnotes

[a] As quoted by Noam Chomsky in *Rogue States* (London: Pluto Press, 2000) p. 4.

[b] For a detailed exposition of this view, see William Robinson, *Promoting Polyarchy: Globalisation, US Intervention and Hegemony* (Cambridge: Cambridge University Press, 1996).

Mindful of the Major Religions

The material in the previous essay about the economic and political power of monopoly capitalism inevitably calls to mind the New Testament dictum that love of money is the root of all evil (I Timothy 5). Quite simply, the multi-national corporations (MNCs) and their political henchmen are motivated by greed, a vice long ago classified by Christianity as one of the seven deadly sins. Further, the MNCs, in seeking economic dominance over the lives of millions of people, are violating the golden rule, as again stated in the New Testament (Matthew 7), of treating others as you would have them treat you.

These references to the religious sphere—they happen to be to Christianity, but they could equally be to the other major religions—clearly show the relevance to the modern world of that sphere's moral perspectives, many of which were articulated over 2,000 years ago. The scriptures of the major religions—Christianity, Judaism, Islam, Hinduism, Buddhism and Zoroastrianism—are united in their censure of avaricious, dominative and selfish impulses: impulses which cause, and have always caused, most of the world's troubles.

Secularists should not be slow to acknowledge the pivotal place occupied by religion in mankind's moral history, even as they rightly reject religion's ontological and cosmological claims. Many, perhaps the majority, of the moral maxims which have exercised universal appeal have found their most memorable expression in religious writings, and recognition of this fact in no way undermines secularism:[1] since, as the atheist Santayana points out, religion has been a prominent field of moral and poetic expression, but one created by man, and therefore no more or less valid than other such fields.[2] The perception that religion, like art and social institutions, is a human construct expressive of moral concerns, allows the secularist to appreciate in full religion's role as one indicator among others

---

[1] Again, a Christian reference is apposite: Christ's words in the Sermon on the Mount (Matthew 5).

[2] Principally in *Reason in Religion* (New York: Dover Publications, 1982 [1905]).

of humanity's main moral propensities and points of sensitivity, its predominant need for harmony and mutuality.

These moral characteristics, the secularist can also point out, are the product of natural selection, and therefore vindicate, not theism, but neo-Darwinism.

The ethical injunctions of the chief religions, in the process of censuring greed, oppression and egotism, convey the general message of moderation in willing, of self restraint and control. It may be argued, indeed, that Hinduism and Buddhism, at least in some of their forms, take this point too far, by advocating the total extinction of willing. But if this is deemed an error, it is at least erring on the right side; and to err on the wrong side, by recommending the complete unleashing of the will, has never been a feature of advanced religious doctrine, just as it has never been present in any moral or social philosophy worthy of the name.

Returning to consideration of the modern world, the twentieth century has provided many examples of the monstrous extremes which human willing can reach when it breaks away from all moral control. Hitler and Stalin are amongst those that spring to mind, but there are also a number of present-day, if smaller-scale, instances as well. In opposing such people, the secularist takes a position which, in terms of principles, has a good deal in common with that of the religionist, while of course differing from the latter in the view taken of the source of those principles. The points of similarity are sufficient for the secularist, when he comprehends the enormous sway that corrupt power holds in the world, to be struck by the force of the statement, in St John's Gospel: 12, that 'the ruler of this world' is Satan. When the statement is de-mythologised, with the Satan-idea replaced by that of human corruptness, it can be seen as a synoptically accurate description of the global state of affairs,[3] and of one calling for action by all morally concerned people.

---

[3] Broadly in this connection, the perennial character of what is generally regarded as evil has been poignantly noted by a number of leading twentieth-century writers, religious and otherwise. These include T. S. Eliot, Jean-Paul Sartre and Eric Heller. Eliot, as a Christian, writes of 'The perpetual struggle of Good and Evil' (*The Rock,* part I), thus echoing not only Christianity but also Zoroastrianism. Sartre, an atheist, speaks in defence of the 'old fashioned categories of Good and Evil' (in his 1952 book on Jean Genet): implying, like Eliot, that evil is an on-going reality. Finally, Heller, writing about the problems faced by the mind which can no longer find sustenance in traditional religion, praises the great nineteenth-century atheists Schopenhauer and Burckhardt for perceiving sin and evil 'as

The MNC issue is clearly relevant here, highlighting as it does the constant problem of greed and acquisitiveness. This problem, incidentally, is also given definitive expression in a non-religious medium: the great novel *Nostromo* (1904) by Joseph Conrad. As one of the novel's characters says: 'There is no peace and rest in the development of material interests.' The material interests of monopoly capital are now the chief factor driving the policies of the world's most powerful governments, and they indeed afford humanity no respite.

In bending swords against such forces, and against the many other evils with which the world is beset, organised secularism advances further along the moral path on which it first embarked in the later nineteenth century. This was the time when the decline of religious belief in the West became decisive. However, despite this decline, secularism inherited a large amount of the moral impetus which had actuated religious believers; hence the frequency of reference, in the secularist literature of the late nineteenth and early twentieth centuries, to the ethical views of Buddha, Jesus and Mohammed. Manifestly, these views had maintained their emotional appeal, even when the ontologies with which they were connected had been refuted and discarded. So to speak, the sun of religious ontology had sunk below the horizon, but the moral after-glow of that sunset still suffused the sky with delicate orange light. Not unlike this should be secularism's present position. In his struggles and strivings, the secularist should draw on the moral heritage from religious culture just as he does on the heritages from other sources, knowing them all to be totally human in origin, significance and application.

---

constituent and ineradicable factors in human history.' See Heller, *The Disinherited Mind* (1952), in the Penguin Books edn 1961, p. 69.

Reading Sartre's 'The Flies'

For the secularist, Sartre's play, first staged in 1942, is a seminal text. It dramatises with great power the experience of breaking free from religious belief and subservience to a theistic mind-set: breaking free in the form of taking decisive action—in this case, an act of assassination. Also dramatised is the sense of self-creation through performing a defiant act: a performance which required overcoming feelings of personal unworthiness and inadequacy.

In addition, there is poignant presentation of the feeling of loneliness, and estrangement from past norms, through acting distinctively and entering uncharted moral terrain. At the same time, counterbalancing this feeling of loneliness is a sense of stability and anchorage in having unequivocally committed oneself through action. Finally, the act of assassination is presented as a free act: free because unconstrained by orthodoxy—because, in fact, a shattering of orthodoxy.

Readers of Sartre will immediately recognise these elements as characteristic of the author's literary work as a whole, and as cornerstones of his philosophy of atheistic existentialism. The latter sees deliberated action as both moral creation and self-creation. Since—it argues—there is no God, moral values do not pre-date humanity as divine fiats awaiting discovery by mankind. On the contrary, values are constructed by human beings, and by them alone, in the making of choices and decisions. They are then fleshed out in action, which therefore extends the creativity that went into the formulation of values. Similarly, selfhood is not a divine creation awaiting discovery by the individual, but something constructed by the latter through the actions he performs.

The majority of secularists will probably concur with almost all these arguments, except perhaps the contention that selfhood is entirely a matter of construction through action. Predominant agreement deepens response to the dramatic power of *The Flies*, which is, incidentally, Sartre's most poetic piece of writing, abounding in vivid images and similes.

Before examining key moments in the text, let's briefly review the plot. Sartre, like a number of French playwrights of his generation, takes material from ancient Greek drama and re-works it to give it specific relevance to modern times. He chooses the story of Orestes's taking revenge on his mother, Clytemnestra, and her lover, Aegisthus, for their murder of his father, Agamemnon. After killing them both, Orestes seeks companionship from his previously supportive sister, Electra, but she feels unable to sustain defiance of the god Zeus's will (which Orestes has transgressed by his action), and refuses companionship. Orestes is left to continue his life alone.

Through this subject-matter, Sartre makes all his main existentialist points, as they apply to Orestes. While it is true that deity does figure in the play, in the form of Zeus, the latter is depicted as a declining force, an old man who relies on burdening human beings with guilt feelings to prevent them from thinking independently, and who proves unable to stop Orestes from taking his revenge and from triumphantly asserting his freedom from divine law. In this way, the whole idea of God is grimly satirised.

Across the unfolding of the play's action are studded Orestes's memorably expressive moments. We first meet him as a rootless wanderer, cultured but anchorless, arriving in the town of Argos unaware that it is here he will perform the defining action of his life. In expressing his feeling of inner emptiness, of having no community or social experience with which he can identify himself, he articulates a desire to fill 'the void within me'. He wishes to fill it with experiences of social involvement, even if these do not entail happiness. This syndrome will be familiar to many highly educated people of today who are conscious of an unfulfilled need for social attachment and commitment.

When it becomes clear to him that Argos is the home of Clyemnestra and Aegisthus, he resolves to take revenge on them, and immediately sees that, with this resolution, his life has been transformed from one of youthful lightness to adult commitment and severity: 'Until now I felt something warm and living round me, like a friendly presence. That something has just died. What emptiness! What emptiness as far as the eye can reach.' Then: 'Give me time to say farewell to all the lightness, the aery lightness that was mine. Let me say good-bye to my youth. There are evenings at Corinth and at Athens, golden evenings full of song and scents and laughter; these I shall never know again.'

Having killed his mother and her lover, and aware that he bears full responsibility for the action by which he has at last defined himself, he avers: 'I have done my deed, Electra, and that deed was good.

I shall bear it on my shoulders as a carrier at a ferry carries the traveller to the farther bank ... The heavier it is to carry, the better pleased shall I be; for that burden is my freedom.'

He later describes himself as 'Beyond anguish and remorse', and rejects Zeus's argument that his action is a crime for which he should repent. In discarding Zeus's laws, he declares that 'I am doomed to have no other law but mine', because 'every man must find out his own way'. When Zeus contends that this path leads only to despair, Orestes retorts with one of Sartre's most famous dictums: 'human life begins on the far side of despair.'

Orestes then exhorts Electra to accompany him on his lonely journey bearing the 'precious load' of his deed. This journey will be 'Towards ourselves. Beyond the rivers and mountains are an Orestes and an Electra waiting for us, and we must make our patient way towards them.' In other words, they must continue the process of creating themselves. When she refuses to accompany him, he realises he must begin entirely alone his 'new life ... A strange life'.

Doubtlessly, many secularists will question the extreme individualism with which Orestes breaks with orthodoxy ('I am doomed to have no other law but my own'). They will argue that moving beyond the constrictions and falsities of theism should always be a communal effort, one creating a new, collective morality. However, while agreeing with this argument, I think we should bear in mind the totality of what Orestes says, conveying as it does the full extent of a *personal experience* of rebellion, defiance and self-defining. It is in depicting a personal experience, as well as a set of personal relationships, that the play works dramatically; and I think we should accept Orestes's extreme individualism as, at least in part, a dramatic ingredient.

Over and above this point, there seems to me no question of the play's general importance to secularism, especially the secular approach to political issues which are deemed to require violence and therefore a defiance of traditional religious attitudes, especially those of Christianity. As Electra says: 'An evil thing is conquered only by another evil thing', and this is unquestionably true in cases where the evil party is unmoved by efforts to return good for evil. Also, this is the view that many secularists, including Sartre himself, took with them into the struggle against Fascism in World War Two: the struggle which was, of course, the context in which *The Flies* was written. It need hardly be added that such a perspective remains central to today's campaigns against oppression and injustice.

The Demise of Absolute Deference

The cess of majesty
Dies not alone, but like a gulf doth draw
What's near it with it; or, 'tis a massy wheel
Fixed on the summit of the highest mount,
To whose huge spokes ten thousand lesser things
Are mortised and adjoined; which when it falls,
Each small annexment, petty consequence,
Attends the boisterous ruin. Never alone
Did the king sigh, but with a general groan.

Hamlet, III.iii.15–23

The view of kingship being expressed here by Shakespeare (and found also in his history plays, especially *Henry V*) was the orthodox one of his day in England. Versions of it, or variants on it, have been the political norm for most of human history. The notion of monarch or ruler as society's centre of gravity and core was the rule in most of the ancient civilisations and, in the West, most regimes up until the end of the eighteenth century.

Almost always, it has been bound up with religious belief, the concepts of deity and human governance being intertwined as, respectively, the force to be served and the means of serving it. About as frequently, it has been found in societies with rigid and long-lasting class differences.

Its decline in the West since the end of the eighteenth century is in fact correlated with the decline of the above conditions, cultural and social, which usually provided its context. The advance of empirical science (and the concomitant growth of technology) plus the weakening of class divisions are the major factors which have republicanised most Western societies; where monarchy remains, it has only figurehead status. This republicanisation has been in tandem with a general liberalisation and emancipation—of thought, expression, way of life. Not that Western society is completely emancipated; this is not, and cannot be, the case while self-interested groups continue to predominate economically, turning democracy toward plutodemocracy. However, despite this predominance, it is still true to say that Western society has been liberated to the point where significant numbers of people regularly question governmental institutions, religious beliefs, social structures, and much else. This questioning, now the norm, was the exception prior to the eighteenth century. Its development confirms the view of Lord Acton—famous, of course, for his dictum that all power tends to corrupt and absolute power corrupts absolutely—that modern history is essentially the story of the emancipation of conscience from authority. As a norm, it continually oils the wheels of intellectual life, so making further radical change an ongoing possibility.

The multi-faceted character of this mental activity means that the political situation conveyed by the words quoted from *Hamlet* will probably never regain a firm foothold in Western societies. That situation, with its social and psychological homogeneity and close-knit unity, belongs to a type of social organisation which precedes or prevents the full development of the scientific and critical mind-sets. Such development abolishes the absolute deference to, and centrality of, political authority as described in *Hamlet.* Instead of a completely centripetal situation, we have one which is part centripetal and part centrifugal. The centrifugal element is constituted by the scientific/critical consciousness, which is in turn made up of the different consciousnesses of all thinking individuals. This wide range of analytical and critical activity renders society psychologically pluralistic and fluid on an unprecedented scale: a scale which shows every sign of being permanent and irreversible. It should be noted that twentieth century attempts at reversal—in the form of totalitarian politics—all failed disastrously. Societies of the modern Western type are, to use Henry James's word, 'headless': a characteristic integral to the type.

Pluralism of response and outlook is the hallmark of what Karl Popper has definitively described as the 'open society', to be differentiated from the 'closed' form which is devoid of extensive critical activity.[a] The 'open society' brings not only intellectual freedom but also intellectual challenges and problems, and these too have been definitively characterised by Popper as the 'strain of civilisation'. This strain is felt by every thinking person as s/he seeks to encompass the unprecedented quantities of information available in the modern world,[1] in the process of trying to achieve viable positions, both ontologically and ethically.

That the psychological fluidity of modern Western societies is not matched by an equal degree of economic fluidity is due to a fact already mentioned: the economic predominance of certain interest-groups. If that predominance can be dismantled, the result should be a further increase in the scope of critical consciousness, a further movement of society away from pre-eighteenth century moulds and mind-sets.

This of course does not mean that society will become utopian. In addition to the problem of the widening of the 'strain of civilisation', there will be other problems, of a traditional character. They will be caused by people totally unaffected by the afore-mentioned strain: extremely wilful and selfish people seeking power either for its own sake or for its economic rewards; or people who, though not power-hungry, are mired in myopic and pedestrian ways of thinking. These groups have never been in short supply, even in periods of major intellectual expansion, and their presence in society must be assumed to be ongoing.

The perspective on the future, not utopianist but meliorist, sees the increasing possibility of establishing a mature and progressive form of anarchy. While contending with regressive groups, forward-looking people have a good chance of creating a society which is in certain key respects completely de-centralised and even de-institutionalised: one where individuals develop themselves and others through the free exchange of ideas, and through voluntary community participation. Each individual values both self-sustenance and fellowship, privacy and public action, his/her own rights and those of others, personal relationships and collective tasks—all the time making uncoerced choices as to involvement. The more extensive those choices, the less need will be felt to defer or refer to authority. Mature anarchy gives people their heads, and looks to their common humanity as a chief source of moral guidance. In other words, it regards them as genuine adults, as individuals who have come of age and are best left to be constructive, creative and associative in their own ways.

In the open society of this kind, centralisation is kept to a necessary minimum, and does not entail intellectual or doctrinal control of any

---

[1] On these quantities, see Andre Malraux's reference to the 'imaginary museum' whose galleries every modern person must comb thoroughly in order to attain judgemental competence.

kind. It simply pursues a set of practical purposes which have been democratically agreed. People look to centralised agencies to meet a relatively small number of expectations, to perform neither more nor less than has been asked of them. Whatever deference is due to them is in strict proportion to their limited remit.

Herbert Spencer famously described the entire process of biological evolution as one in which matter passes from 'an indefinite, incoherent homogeneity to a definite, coherent heterogeneity'.[b] The same, broadly speaking, could be said of the changes which have taken place in Western society chiefly since the eighteenth century. The 'indefinite, incoherent homogeneity' is reflected partly in the *Hamlet* passage previously quoted, but more so in *Henry V*, which depicts a large number of the poor coming together to serve the monarch in a politically unquestioning way, and without having a clear sense of their social identity or any civil rights other than the minimum guaranteed by common law. The waning in the West of the play's Elizabethan concept of authority over the last three centuries[2] has gradually produced a 'definite coherent heterogeneity', with the emergence of various social groups who have a clear sense of collective identity and possess a range of civil and political rights. The aim should be to develop this heterogeneity even further, and to give its coherence an increasingly anarchical character, along the lines previously sketched.

---

[2] It should of course be noted that the waning process began in England in the mid-seventeenth century, well over a hundred years before the American and French Revolutions. The radical reduction in monarchical power secured by the defeat of Charles I in the English Civil War of the 1640s marked the final overthrowal of the Elizabethan concept of kingship in this country. This achievement put England historically far ahead of almost all of the rest of Western Europe, and was therefore exceptional both for its own century and for most of the next. Also, it is significant that this political radicalism was matched by major advances in science and philosophy: intellectually, England was a European leader in the seventeenth century.

Endnotes

[a] See *The Open Society and its Enemies*, first published 1945.

[b] As quoted by Will Durant in *The Story of Philosophy*, p. 319.

Economic Activity as Part of a Greater Whole

The view of economic activity as only part of a larger way of relating to others in society is one found in many previous and contemporary cultures, especially those of a religious kind (including so-called 'archaic' cultures with religious creeds). However, this view barely obtains, at least at the public level, in societies which are extensively capitalistic and which therefore emphasise economic competition. Such societies may, in various ways or degrees, be religious (see for example Weber and Tawney on the links between Protestantism and capitalism); but, where so, their religious component is insufficient to produce the pervasive and deeply comforting sense of fellowship, the widespread feelings of calm, trust and joy in the presence of others, which are engendered by religion at its (admittedly occasional) best. Such edification is of course available to the secular mind as well as to the religious—in fact more so, secularists will aver; but, whatever the mind-set, the profoundly satisfying emotions we have been describing are clearly marginal where daily life is dominated by economic competition, strife and mistrust.

Capitalism, at least in its modern monopoly form, has probably done more than any other system to separate economic activity from the other key spheres of human life. There are of course variations within capitalism; for instance, Japanese and German practice is regarded as being less separatist than Anglo-American; but, overall, the system has been culturally divisive to an unprecedented extent. This is true not only of the societies which originated capitalism but also of those on which it was subsequently imposed.

Arguments for the dismantling of monopoly capitalism have previously been advanced. My view is that such dismantling is a necessary condition for re-connecting economic activity to the other activities which are vital for human well-being, integration and comradeship. (At the same time, there is no need to end capitalism in all its forms; provided its province is confined to small-scale enterprise occupying a limited space in the economy, it will not have the massively fragmenting effect it has had thus far.)

The demise of monopoly capitalism is a prerequisite for the full and free exchange of ideas and opinions throughout society. The wielding of large-scale economic power militates against intellectual freedom. Liberty includes the right to question, or even say 'no' to, the powerful boss, and that right is difficult to exercise when the boss holds the purse-strings. Liberty also includes open access to public outlets for the expression of ideas, and this access is severely limited when big business either controls or influences most of those outlets.

The issue of access is particularly important in relation to original and radical developments in the arts and philosophy. Here, a general point about intellectual emancipation can be made. This emancipation should go hand in hand with liberation from oppressive economic structures. There is no point opposing such structures and at the same time attempting to impose closure on people's outlooks by, for example, advocating a cult of ordinariness and averageness, and of rigid 'class' affiliation. This advocacy is unfortunately found among some groups on the political Left. Emancipation means release from *all* constrictions on full human flourishing, on people exercising the complete range of cultural choice and on realising their various capacities to the full. It means, in other words, cultural pluralism. Only under pluralism can true intellectual freedom obtain.

In a society free of the current restrictions on the flow of ideas and opinions, economic activity would not be seen, as much of it is now, as a hiatus in intellectual and emotional vitality, a block on the metabolism of the higher mental and affective faculties, and therefore as something which prevents the full realisation of people's capacities to communicate with and respond to each other, in the course of the daily round. Admittedly, the working relations entailed by any economic system are in general less profound than the personal relations existing outside the work-context; but even so, much can still be done to make the former more meaningful, in terms of growth of mutual understanding and of relating work to society's larger cultural and ethical concerns. Inadequate effort, or complete absence of effort, to deepen work-relations in these ways results in the attitudes of alienation and even cynicism which are unfortunately (if unofficially) widespread in modern society.

This issue of attitude is especially relevant to secularism, which, unlike most religious culture, does not offer a supernaturalistic and transcendental perspective in which to place work-activity. Its perspective being wholly naturalistic and immanent, it must emphasise the value of work as a fundamental aspect of human fellowship—that fellowship which, as William Morris says, is 'life' itself. Too often, a division is drawn between work and life: between, on the one hand, working and, on the other, living in the fullest sense.[1] Again, while there are many significant experiences which cannot be accessed within the work-context, there remain many that can, if the attitude is appropriate, and these should never be underestimated.

For the secularist, the main business of human beings is to share with each other as widely as is possible. (It is of course acknowledged that the possible degree of sharing varies, depending on the individuals concerned.) Every constructive human energy should be channelled into a common pool constituting a collective ethical and cultural dynamism: a dynamism valued for breaking new ground. Such vitality and creativity have, for secularism, an ultimate status.

---

[1] The reference to Morris inevitably reminds us of other nineteenth-century figures who sought to make work-activity a genuine 'life' activity. These include Carlyle and Ruskin. Overall, nineteenth-century writing on this subject remains a major source of illumination.

Emile Durkheim

Achieving Moral Consensus in Modern Society

This text is reproduced by kind permission of the editor of the journal *The Ethical Record.*

Emile Durkheim (1858–1917) is one of a number of distinguished French sociologists of the last 200 years; among others are Montesquieu, Comte and Tocqueville. This essay will consist of a —necessarily brief—exposition of his main ideas on the subject of moral consensus. In a short, final section, I will attempt some commentary, in connection with certain personal views I have on the recent and present state of British society (as an example of the modern Western type of collectivity about which Durkheim wrote). Also, exposition of Durkheim's view will be given in the past tense, whereas what I regard as incontrovertibly or arguably fact will be stated in the present tense.

For Durkheim, the achievement of moral consensus was a key issue. Consensus is of course vital for all societies, but, as Durkheim argued, especially so in the modern Western context. This was the case because modern society had a form of solidarity which was *organic,* as distinct from *mechanical.* Organic solidarity was a kind which achieved unity and harmony through differentiation, diversity, and the extensive development of individuality. By contrast, mechanical solidarity rested not on difference but on resemblance: its unity depended on individuals closely resembling one another, and sharing, almost entirely, the same general outlook. (This distinction, incidentally, recalls Popper's between open and closed societies. It's worth noting that Durkheim's precedes Popper's.)

Durkheim chose the term 'organic' with a biological analogy in mind. Organic social solidarity worked in the way an animal body does: different organs perform different functions to maintain an overall, co-ordinated metabolism.

He added that mechanical solidarity was characteristic of what sociologists call archaic societies—those without writing—while organic solidarity, as said, characterised modern Western society. Historically, the mechanical came first, and the organic arose with the disintegration of the former.

However, in all societies, the organic no less than the mechanical, there existed a collective consciousness of some kind. While there was a contrast in the degree to which the collective outlook influenced that of the individual in mechanical and organic societies, nevertheless the person in the organic context was, in considerable measure, tied to the social whole. Though, in mechanical solidarity, the collective mind filled the major part of the individual's perspective, whereas in organic solidarity it occupied much less space, still the person in the organic context was required to adhere to a number of collective norms, albeit far fewer than in the mechanical context. This was the case in spite of the differentiation between individuals which Durkheim saw as the defining feature of organic solidarity; and despite the fact that, under organic conditions, the individual was to a large extent free to believe, desire and act according to his/her own preferences.

For Durkheim, the individual was always inseparable from the group; s/he was in fact born of society; society was not born of individuals. Society formed the individual, and was not formed by individuals. The social whole was always greater than its parts, with a character distinct from the characters of its individual members. Accordingly, the whole explained the parts, and not the converse. Social facts were accounted for by other social facts, and not by facts of individual psychology. In order to understand the status of the individual in society, one had to examine the collectivity which made that status possible. (This subordination of part to whole echoes Hegel's social philosophy.)

To illustrate his thesis, Durkheim pointed out that, in modern society, differentiation between individuals goes hand in hand with an extensive division of labour. He went on to argue that such diversity was partly the result of the division of labour, but also partly a cause of it. Indeed, it was mainly cause, since the whole idea of extensive division of work would have been inconceivable in a society which did not *already possess* a highly developed sense of individuality, and was not, therefore, already organic in character. Hence the emergence of a widespread variegation of labour reflected an already-existing organic solidarity, though one that would develop further. Hence also, the division of labour extended differentiation but did not create it.

To illustrate these general points: in order to comprehend the role that contracts play in modern society, we had to understand that contractual practice between individuals or small groups was itself made possible by the overall structure of the society in which those individuals and groups lived. This was a structure shaped by a collective consciousness which had a particular sense of right and wrong, justice and injustice, and which had formulated a legal system sanctioning contracts. The collective consciousness was, again, of the organic type, allowing individuals to do things, such as drawing up contracts, which they would not have been allowed to do had the collectivity been mechanical. Once more, then, the practice of particular individuals was enabled by conditions which the individuals themselves did not create. (All this runs counter to some traditional liberal schools of social thought, especially those connected with social-contract theory.)

Thus for Durkheim there were three main points to note about modern organic society: (1) It was highly differentiated: a fact which, as said, was its defining feature. (2) This differentiation was nevertheless the expression of a collective outlook which sanctioned individuality. (3) Because the collective outlook was the condition for individualism, the latter could never be absolute, if society was to hold together. The collectivity placed necessary limits on the sphere of individual conduct; it imposed responsibilities and prohibitions, in addition to granting extensive freedoms. Further, it transmitted a moral and cultural heritage which occupied a significant space in the individual mentality, no matter how distinctive the latter might be.

Organic society, then, tempered individualism by possessing a number of beliefs, feelings and values which were common to all its members. Or—at least—such was the case when society was in a healthy condition, with a balanced relationship between the individual and the group. But unfortunately this balance did not always obtain. It broke down when the individual demanded more of society than the latter could give, and when the ties binding the individual to the group were too weak. This lack of cohesion was defined by Durkheim as *anomie*: absence of regulative norms. The psychological consequences of *anomie* could be profound, including the kind of suicide which Durkheim describes as anomic.

In such conditions—and for Durkheim they were always potential, where not actual, in modern society—the question arose: how can the individual be sufficiently integrated into the whole? In seeking an answer, Durkheim considered the institutions of the family, the state and the religious group. All three he rejected as inadequate. The family unit was in decline in modern society, in terms of both its moral and economic influence on the individual. The state, or rather the political machinery of the state, was simply too remote from most individuals. The religious group was also insufficient: it no longer exercised the degree of moral discipline over its members that it once had done. Also, religious doctrines were wilting under the attack from science; and Durkheim regarded science as the only valid form of ontological thinking.[1]

Durkheim concluded that the only group which could adequately integrate the individual was the professional organisation: what he called the 'corporation'. Corporations, in the form he envisaged, would include employers and employees. They would be close enough to the individual—in terms of work—to provide a school of discipline, and far enough above him/her to enjoy (as employer) prestige and authority. More will be said later on this subject.

The urgency with which Durkheim pursued his solution to the problem of integration reflects his larger view that some form of fundamental commitment to society had to replace previous commitments to religion. Such commitment was a moral necessity; and it was—in the modern scientific era—the natural metamorphosis of its religious predecessors. Science, specifically anthropology and sociology, had shown that the religious impulse was at bottom a social impulse, that religions had an essentially social nature, served social needs, and that 'Religious interests are merely the symbolic expression of social and moral interests.'[a] (See Feuerbach and Santayana, among others, for identical views.) In attaching himself to those interests, the individual experienced a sense of transcendence, of being part of something greater than himself. This 'something greater' was a natural phenomenon—human society in all its complexity—and not anything supernatural. The individual's feeling of allegiance to the human collective was the naturalistic and wholly justifiable successor to the supernaturalistic notion of transcendence, which was now totally outmoded. Duty to society would come to be seen as something sacred, and as completely separate from the profane and banal routines involved in the narrow pursuit of self-interest and merely egocentric goals.

---

[1] This view of science will be, for secularists, non-controversial. However, Durkheim goes on to make a highly controversial claim: that science can itself provide moral guidance.

(However, a key question is raised by this view: was Durkheim talking in real or ideal terms when he spoke of society's warranting a sacred sense of commitments? Did he mean society as it was or is, or society as it might or should be? It is probably uncontentious to say that societies thus far in human history have always left a great deal to be desired, and therefore have not deserved the reverence which Durkheim advocated. Was he then speaking in ideal terms? This is a question to which his writings provide no clear answer.)

Duty to society, Durkheim went on to stress, was a matter of consensus. (In the emphasis he placed on this term, he echoes Comte.) Consensus was in turn a matter of socialisation: the integration and moralisation of the individual. In insisting on the primary importance of these processes, Durkheim saw himself as a 'socialist', but a socialist of an unusual stamp. 'Integrationism' is perhaps a better word for the kind of socialism he espoused. This is definitely not the socialism of Marx, and for three reasons. Firstly, Durkheim did not favour violence as a means of achieving social change. Secondly, he did not regard class struggle as an essential element in modern society, or as the impetus of the movement of history. Lastly, he saw the social problem as moral more than economic; in other words, it would not be solved merely by economic measures. For Durkheim, conflicts of a class and economic nature, while undeniably real, were themselves symptoms of a deeper problem: that of a fundamental loss of harmony and mutuality in social relations, a state of *anomie*. It was this that needed to be put right before other, more technical programmes of action could be fruitfully undertaken. What first had to be attained was a more intelligent and humane organisation of collective life, one which integrated individuals within communities that were invested with moral authority, and which fulfilled an educational role.

Durkheim saw socialist doctrines of the more conventional type as missing the essential point about the primary need for moral integration. He argued that conventional modern socialism, as distinct from the communistic doctrines which have existed throughout history, regarded economic activity and productivity as fundamental. It sought, not the simple and frugal life-style associated with traditional communism, but material abundance and the full development of productive capacities. Yet this abundance, Durkheim added, was not in itself a guarantor of social harmony: it might, in fact, lead to conflict, by failing to appease the economic appetites it aroused in individuals. (In his grasp of the problem of unbridled individual drives, Durkheim recalls Hobbes.) Harmony could only come from a sphere external and prior to the economic: the sphere, as said, of moral and educational frameworks.

Durkheim alleged that conventional socialism failed to recognise the importance of this non-economic sphere, and that this basic error led to what he called the anarchic tendencies of socialist doctrine. He insisted that economic functions needed to be subjected to an over-arching authority that was both moral and political. His view was that, before the emergence of modern industrial society, economic functions had been subordinated to supra-economic powers, and that a modern equivalent to these powers had to be constructed. (We might ask: are these criticisms of socialism fair? Are socialists preoccupied with economics, and neglectful of extra-economic, moral, cultural and political considerations? Many would reply that the neglect lies not with them but with *laissez faire* capitalism at its worst.)

Durkheim's concern with the extra-economic brings us back to what was said earlier about the role he wished to assign to professional organisations or 'corporations'. The latter would possess the social and moral authority requisite for exerting control over economic life, and for preventing individuals from yielding to the infinity of their desires.

Further, they would serve as intermediaries between the individual and the state. Like Tocqueville, Durkheim saw a major danger in the growth of state power on the one hand, and the increasing political isolation of the individual on the other. Also, as we have seen, he viewed the modern state as too remote from the individual to be an agency of social integration.

Additional to Durkheim's focus on professional organisations was his concern for democracy. This is clearly evident in his afore-mentioned fear about the growth of state power. He saw democracy less in terms of political mechanisms than of states of mind. Here, we return to the subject of the collective consciousness, with which the individual consciousness was imbued. Durkheim writes:

> A nation is more democratic to the extent that deliberation, reflection and the critical spirit play a more important role in the progress of public affairs. It is less democratic to the extent that ignorance, unacknowledged habits, obscure feelings – in short, unexamined prejudices – are preponderant ... In other words, democracy is not a discovery or rediscovery of our century; it is the character increasingly assumed by societies ... its rise has been continuous from the beginning of history.[b]

By implication, the development of a democratic collective mind is co-extensive with the development of science. Moreover for Durkheim, this type of consciousness played three key roles: first, it underpinned the political order which he deemed indispensable to society. Next, as a consequence of this, it enlarged genuine communication between the body-politic and the population as a whole. Thirdly, as in turn a consequence of this, it strengthened the individual's sense of belonging to a particular kind of community: in effect, an open society. (Again, echoes of Popper.)

This latter point returns us to the central issue of the individual and the group. The combination in democracy of order and freedom involved for Durkheim the principle that the individual should willingly submit to control or discipline as a pre-condition for his and everyone else's personal development. Limits had to be set to each individual sphere so that all individual spheres could have space to develop.

The above argument clearly connects with the basic Durkheimian tenet that the social is always prior to the individual. Regarding individual freedom specifically, this was a social product: 'liberty has become a reality only in and through society'.[c]

Insistence on the anteriority of the group to the individual did not, however, lead Durkheim to an undervaluing of the latter. As said, he prized social discipline partly as a means of maximising individual development. Further, throughout his work, he viewed differentiation as a fortunate and desirable development in human history. Increasing range of occupation, life-style, cultural orientation, initiative, self-accountability and rationality: all were seen as healthy phenomena. In fact, Durkheim regarded individualist, rationalist, liberal thought as the final term in man's social and historical evolution. In this respect, he presented a kind of 'end of intellectual history' scenario, delineating a stage beyond which humanity could not and need not go. This stage was ultimate because, among other things, it maximised opportunity for scientific and critical activity. His conception of a final intellectual condition for mankind is of course not to be confused with the possession of a final ontological perspective. It is simply the condition of complete intellectual openness. As such, it is surely one which all secularists and liberal-rationalists will endorse.

At the same time, as we have seen, Durkheim was keenly aware of the problems that accompany an effluorescence of individualist thought: *anomie,* inter-individual tension and conflict. He noted that there is no evidence that people are on balance happier in organic societies than in mechanical ones—even if they are more free. He was fully aware, in a manner which recalls Sartre and (once more) Popper, of the burdens of individual freedom and choice. His grasp of the problematic led him, as noted, to stress the importance of social consensus, cohesion and collective norms: these were just as important as personal freedom. Hence his perspective is a delicate balance between the claims of the individual and those of the group. He desired a society which was committed to both individual fulfilment and to general stability.

The balance Durkheim sought—and let's remember that he died as long ago as 1917—is one which modern Western society has still not achieved. It is probably true that this equilibrium has never been fully realised, and perhaps never will be: see what was said earlier about the social situation's always leaving much to be desired. However, the balance remains an ideal toward which to approximate. Hence it is worth looking at recent times to see how they have measured up in this respect.

It's arguable that, in the 1980s and most of the 90s, British society as a whole swung too far in the individualistic direction, to the detriment of collective norms. Phrases such as 'the Me-generation' and assertions such as 'there is no such thing as society' reflected this tendency, tied up as it was with material acquisitiveness and the view that politics has far less to do with moral principles or ideology than with increasing the sphere of affluence. Conspicuously lacking was the kind of moral connectedness, over and above economics, which Durkheim advocated. Equally lacking were large-scale outlets to satisfy the need for intense collective commitment. It will be recalled that Durkheim regarded this need as the effective foundation of traditional religion, and as one which—being perennial—now had to be met in secular, wholly societal ways.

There are currently signs that society is moving toward a more balanced position *vis à vis* the individual and the group. Since the late 90s, we have seen a growth in large-scale collective involvement, one that includes a radical questioning of, rather than acquiescence in, the economic and political *status quo*. Examples of this involvement are the movements against economic globalisation and against what is seen as Western imperialism in the Middle East. Also, at a smaller-scale and local level, and actually over a longer period, there has been a growth in communitarianism, voluntary social activism, and other initiatives to bring individuals together in morally constructive and mutually strengthening ways. All these tendencies are notable for by-passing the institutional and bureaucratic rigidities of local and national government. They are offering a genuine locus for integration and sharing. It is to be hoped that this locus will continue to widen.

On the other hand, we have not seen a similar expansion of the integrative role of professional and occupational organisations. Durkheim, as said, placed his main hope in such an expansion. Employer-employee contexts have not in general kept pace with the informal ones previously specified. This may be precisely because of the character of the latter: being informal, they offer much greater scope for the untrammelled exchange of ideas, attitudes, feelings, and cultural perspectives, than is normally possible between employers and their staff. This discrepancy between the specifically occupational and the generally societal has become even more marked with the growth of technocratic occupations. Also, while it is true that some professions – for example, law, teaching, medicine, social work – do have a strong moral component and social orientation, they account for only a minority of the working population, given the specialist abilities and qualifications they require. Hence only a small proportion of employees can directly benefit from the ethical frameworks they provide.

What is generally needed to reduce this discrepancy is greater linkage for the individual between job and broad social involvement, between work-relations and relations to society as a whole, between earning a living and participating in a common pursuit that is both moral and cultural. In this regard, we might remember E. M. Forster's previously quoted dictum, 'Only connect.'

Most conventional socialists argue that this linkage can indeed be established with a transformation in the economic system. They insist that, under capitalism, employer–employee relations cannot possibly have the integrative function that Durkheim wished for them. These points obviously relate to socialism's argument about the essential alienation of workers in the capitalist system. The socialist line of thinking is certainly an important one, and in some economic respects is more realistic than Durkheim's. However, the point about alienation applies mainly to industrial production, which in modern society is of course only one of many areas of occupational activity. Also, we should recall Durkheim's fundamental criticism of conventional socialism: that it paid insufficient attention to non-economic factors, and wrongly assumed that problems of social integration were largely economic in character, and were therefore soluble wholly within the economic sphere. How far this criticism is justified is open to question. What is certain, however, is that contemporary society – despite some growth in cohesiveness – is faced with a plethora of social difficulties which economic measures alone will not solve. They are so deeply matters of culture, environment, inheritance from the past, general morality and interpersonal relations, that many approaches in addition to economic ones are required. Hence Durkheim's emphasis on the extra-economic remains seminal.

Finally, reflecting on the entire range of Durkheim's arguments, issues of agreement and disagreement are to some extent secondary to the basic fact that he obliges secularists to look long and hard at general social questions, and to see them as central and inescapable. After reading Durkheim, a purely private form of secularism is no longer possible. By drawing attention to the never-ceasing link between the collective and the individual, the social and the personal, Durkheim achieves at least two things. First, he reminds us of our social responsibilities, especially to those who need our help. Second, by showing us how, as individuals, we are inextricably located within social formations, he helps us deal with problems of personal loneliness and atomisation: problems which are in fact widespread. As we become more aware of our relatedness to society, we become more appreciative of the latter and all it has to offer; and, in turn, more conscious of what we can contribute toward it. Thus we reject absolutely the contention that 'there is no such thing as society'.

For the secularist, one's fellow human beings are the only agency of support. These are not just family and friends but also the wider collective. The secular view that our fellows are all we have to rely on is powerfully reinforced by the rich and variegated character of Durkheim's work.

Endnotes

[a] As quoted by Raymond Aron, in his section on Durkheim in *Main Currents in Sociological Thought 2* (1967), in the Pelican Books edn, 1970, p. 52.

[b] *Ibid.*, p. 92.

[c] *Ibid.*, p. 101.

[d] Durkheim's main works are: (1) *On the Division of Labour;* (2) *Suicide*; (3) *The Elementary Forms of Religious Life;* (4) *The Rules of Sociological Method.*

Russell and Santayana

At the Threshold of the Twentieth Century

This text is reproduced by kind permission of the editor of the journal *The Ethical Record*.

First of all, let's consider what it meant, for the advanced Western mind, to stand at the threshold of the twentieth century. The nineteenth century had witnessed unparalleled advances in the sciences, and these had inevitably produced profound repercussions in philosophy. They had also massively weakened the ontological claims of Christianity, traditionally the West's major religion. Perhaps the most famous example of this undermining effect was the impact of Darwinism and evolutionary biology; but on all scientific fronts the assault on Christian ontology was formidable. Overall, the intellectual changes wrought in the nineteenth century made it the first century in modern Western history whose leading thinkers were predominantly and overtly agnostic or atheistic. Schopenhauer, Marx, Feuerbach, Buchner, von Hartmann, and Nietzsche in Germany; Bentham, Mill, Huxley, Tyndall, Clifford and Spencer in England; Comte in France: these men, with their radically challenging perspectives, were characteristic of the nineteenth century as their religious contemporaries were not. Some exerted widespread influence not only in philosophy but also literature. In fact, the general intellectual atmosphere they created has remained characteristic of advanced Western culture; it prevails today, in advanced circles, just as it did, in the same circles, during the twentieth century.

It was this atmosphere that nurtured Bertrand Russell and George Santayana. Santayana, born 1863, and Russell, born 1872, came to intellectual maturity in the closing part of the nineteenth century, at a time when the momentum accumulated by the secular thinking of their predecessors was at its height. Respect for science, rationalism and open enquiry was, among exploring minds, at high tide.

However, this respect was exacting, as it always is. Liberation from the mental shackles of a supernaturalistic outlook was of course exhilarating, but it was replaced by the exigencies of a scientific world view which saw the cosmos as godless, mindless, purposeless, and mankind as a minute, fragile feature of the cosmic totality. The disintegration of religious illusions about man's origin and place in the universe left a grim perspective in which humanity was seen as a marginal and transient element in the continuing, wholly mechanistic changefulness of the cosmos. Both Russell and Santayana bore the full weight of this perspective, and unflinchingly explored its implications.

At the same time, they sought sustenance in the face of grimness: they looked to certain kinds of human association, shared activities and goals, which could provide inspiration and comfort without illusions, without any falsification of reality. Their engagement with both the negative and positive ramifications of a scrupulously scientific approach to the universe is, clearly, as relevant now as it was 100 years ago.

That engagement is definitively expressed by Russell in an essay published in 1903, entitled 'A free man's worship'; and by Santayana in an essay published in 1900 called 'A religion of disillusion'. The Russell essay originally appeared in a journal called *The Independent Review*, and was later reprinted in Russell's book *Mysticism and Logic* (1917). The Santayana essay appeared in his book *Interpretations of Poetry and Religion* (as above, 1900). The closeness of the publication dates seems, in retrospect, highly significant, as if the two philosophers, though of course working entirely separately, were jointly presenting themselves as the inheritors of the nineteenth-century secular achievement: an inheritance which they had filtered through the medium of their own sensibilities, and were now passing on to the twentieth century, having infused it with their own personal colouring.

Let's begin with 'A free man's worship'. Russell avers:

> That Man is the product of causes which had no prevision of the end they were achieving; that his origin, his growth, his hopes and fears, his loves and his beliefs, are but the outcome of accidental collocations of atoms; that no fire, no heroism, no intensity of thought and feeling, can preserve an individual life beyond the grave; that all the labours of the ages, all the devotion, all the inspiration, all the noonday brightness of human genius, are destined to extinction in the vast death of the solar system, and that the whole temple of Man's achievement must inevitably be buried beneath the debris of a universe in ruins – all these things, if not quite beyond dispute, are yet so nearly certain that no philosophy which rejects them can hope to stand.

In the process of referring to astronomy's prediction that the sun will eventually self-destruct, a prediction already well established by the turn of the twentieth century, Russell powerfully conveys the afore-mentioned sense of man as an ephemeral and fortuitous episode in a fundamentally non-human march of cosmic events: as a passing phase of the solar system's ultimately supra-human momentum.

This view finds a striking parallel in Santayana's words in 'A religion of disillusion'. Man's fortuitous status is captured in Santayana's definition of humanity as 'the product and the captive of an irrational engine called the universe'. Mankind's peripheral position in a cosmos which pursues its own course regardless of humanity is emphasised when Santayana says: 'That Nature is immense, that her laws are mechanical, that the existence and wellbeing of man upon the earth are, from the point of view of the universe, an indifferent incident—all this is ... to be clearly recognised.'

The essay goes on to describe the human mind from a naturalistic standpoint. Man's intelligence is seen as the product of particular biological conditions, conditions which necessarily delimit it. The mind can never know more than it is biologically capable of knowing, can never transcend the context from which it originated; and since that context is but a small and transitory part of the stupendous physical evolution of the universe, intellect is, by its very nature, incapable of knowing all—or, at least, all about the future. To be omniscient, it would have to stand above space and time, as something wholly non-contingent, wholly independent of physical circumstances. The contrary being the case, the person of naturalistic outlook will recognise the futility of striving for omniscience and 'will silence the demands of his own reason and call them chimerical'. Ultimate ignorance and universal mutability are the realities he will accordingly resign himself to.

Russell too is keenly aware of the limitations imposed on the mind by humanity's physical situation. In 'A free man's worship', he speaks of man's 'brief years' and 'little day'—in which, however, he may try to garner as much knowledge as his situation allows. At the same time, there is in Russell, though not in Santayana, a sense of the cosmos as a place of darkness, despite its many suns. He refers to those people who have shed the illusions bred by Christian ontology, and are therefore bereft of the false certainties which accompany those illusions, as 'fellow sufferers in the same darkness'. Further, mankind is seen as positioned on a narrow raft surrounded by 'the dark ocean on whose rolling waves we toss for a brief hour'. The raft itself is illumined only by 'the flickering light of human comradeship'. (Incidentally, in the use he makes of the idea of darkness, Russell is remarkably similar to James Thomson, in his famous poem *The City of Dreadful Night*, published thirty years before 'A free man's worship'.)

Santayana's way of describing the cosmos is less dramatic, but equally gaunt. He speaks of 'the intractable infinite', of 'the blind energy behind Nature', and of the universe apart from humanity as 'a chaos'.

It is clear that much of the above, both in substance and tone, anticipates the writings of the atheistic existentialists in a later part of the twentieth century, especially Sartre and Camus. There are also echoes backwards, particularly of Schopenhauer and Nietzsche.

Given this daunting viewpoint, Russell and Santayana sought, as said, support and inspiration from wholly human sources. Supernaturalistic categories of all kinds were eschewed. In Russell, there is a call to assert human solidarity, and to maintain compassionate and civilised values in the face of a brute universe devoid of them. In Santayana, the argument is similar but more extensive, urging the creation of a specifically human order—social, artistic, scientific—as a riposte to the outer cosmic chaos. In these views, contemporary humanism is prefigured: the perspective of all present-day humanists is that mankind can establish and maintain its context only as something distinct from the surrounding cosmos.

Let's now look in more detail at Russell's position. He begins by emphasising the limitations within which humanity must work to construct its habitation. The harsh truths revealed by astronomy are the 'scaffolding', the inescapable parameters, which set the boundaries to such construction. The recognition of these parameters, and of the non-moral character of the omnipotent cosmic processes, must both be continually borne in mind as humanity goes about the task of creating moral and psychological anchorage for itself. Russell argues that full acknowledgement of limits will lead to a renunciation of desire for personal goods, since the latter are 'subject to the mutations of Time'. Renunciation is also called for by the recognition that 'the world was not made for us'. This attitude should, he says, be shared by all people of panoramic outlook. (One might add that the call for renunciation carries obvious echoes of the asceticism traditionally associated with religious culture. But we should remember that asceticism has been as much a part of general philosophical culture as of religious. In this case, it is humanistic.)

Russell goes on to say that renunciation is not in fact an end in itself but a path 'to the daylight of wisdom, by whose radiance a new insight, a new joy, a new tenderness, shine forth to gladden the pilgrim's heart'. (Again, in the diction, note echoes of religious culture, but also the applicability to humanism.) This inspiring and sustaining outlook is actually a state of mental mastery over 'the thoughtless forces of Nature'. By understanding these forces fully, by perceiving even their physical superiority, one achieves mental superiority over them. They are cognitively absorbed, assimilated, placed, and so lose the power to terrify and dismay. Likewise the sorrow and pain with which human life is fraught: 'to feel these things and to know them is to conquer them'.

The internal victory over the adversity of external fact constitutes a kind of cognitive heroism, and is 'the true baptism into the glorious company of heroes, the true initiation into the over-mastering beauty of human existence'. That beauty includes the great achievements in the arts and sciences—the work, indeed, of 'the noon-day brightness of human genius' to which Russell has previously referred. This is a beauty everyone can avail himself/herself of.

From psychological triumph over external adversity comes not only renunciation and wisdom but also 'charity'; 'with their birth, a new life begins'. The new life means 'to burn with passion for eternal things', and so gain a freedom which attachment to the merely personal and temporary can never give. Such burning is in fact 'the free man's worship'. In these words, we are inevitably reminded of Spinoza and his concept of *sub specie aeternitatis*. Spinoza was actually a major influence on Russell, though he is not mentioned in 'A free man's worship'.

Pervading this whole mind-set is a panoramic joy and happiness which is fully deserved because it has a valid ontological foundation. Scientifically endorsed, hard-won, purified, it is the rightful reward of everyone who has consistently trod the scientific path and steadily shed illusions. That path constantly demands toil, is constantly upward, and is unsparing in many of the vistas it unfolds. At the same time, being equal to its exigencies is a source of profound satisfaction: possessing the unflagging zeal to move higher and higher is the foundation of happiness and the essence of the free man's worship.

The idea of moral and cultural sharing which runs through Russell's thinking is taken substantially further in Santayana. Once, he says, humanity has realised that, outside the human sphere, all is alien, chaotic and beyond control, it should aim to create and maintain order in the small physical region it occupies. If the extra-human area is chaos, in the sense of being purposeless, then the human area may be made a cosmos – meaning, as in the original Greek sense of the word, a purposively ordered system. Though human evolution is founded on the aimlessness and non-rationality which underlie all physical facts in the universe, man can give that non-rationality a conscious direction and aim. Through the exercise of intelligence, he can bring satisfaction and fulfilment to the energies which, having come into being blindly, precede intelligence. In thus rationalising the pre-rational, humanity creates 'the cosmos of society, character and art' – indeed, the whole realm of culture and civilisation. Metaphorically speaking, this cosmos is 'a Noah's ark floating in the Deluge' or 'an oasis ... in Nature'.

In examining the benefits of such order within chaos, Santayana puts considerable emphasis on equanimity. Once, he feels, man has properly understood his place in nature, he will attain peace with himself, and at the same time make peace with the crude forces that surround him. Having established his province and differentiated himself from the rest of the universe, he will have no desire to sink back to the mindless turbulence from which he first emerged, and out of which he has, with great difficulty, managed to raise himself.

Also, in achieving inner peace, he will take an objective view of the whole range of his volitions, and so be better able to satisfy them in an intelligent, circumspect manner. This objectivity will be instinct with the naturalistic perspective, and so will ensure that men do not regard their will as having a sacred character or supernatural source.

The constructing of the human cosmos is 'the building of our own house', the race's way of achieving 'something like its perfection and its ideal', under planetary conditions which constitute a fortuitous equilibrium of natural forces favourable to that advanced form of animal evolution that is mankind. This equilibrium, though accidental, has proved long-lasting, and may well be 'no less stable than that which keeps the planets revolving in their orbits'. (Santayana does not here refer to the prediction about the sun's self-destruction, though he does elsewhere in his work.) Thus civilisation 'need not be short-lived'.

Nevertheless, such a balance of forces is only culture's necessary condition. Its sufficient condition is the human willingness and resolve to create it – 'for there is none other that builds it for us'.

Civilisation is up to us, not to some superhuman agency. Only by understanding this in all its implications can we make 'that rare advance in wisdom which consists in abandoning our illusions the better to attain our ideals'.

Throughout 'A religion of disillusion', Santayana maintains a distinctive note of sobriety and restraint. Recognising the contingent and accidental character of human existence, and confronting the vastness and indifference of nature, he recommends 'patience and dignity'. He emphasises the need to avoid unrealistic hopes and excessive or misplaced enthusiasm. One of the many strengths of his writing in general is its effect of radically disciplining mind and emotion.

We might add that the world could do with far more of the restraint he advocates, because it would reduce violence and the threat of it. The century at the start of which Santayana wrote has been the most murderous on record. It has been fraught with killing produced, for the most part, by conflicts with roots in rigid ideology, nationalism and ethnicism. These conflicts could, in the main, have been resolved peacefully if human beings had had a wider scientific sense of themselves: a sense of common evolutionary origin and of shared vulnerability as members of a hard-pressed species which is alone—as far as present knowledge shows—in a universe which knows it not.

The same point can of course be made in connection with Russell's advocacy of wisdom and charity. It even relates to his recommendation of renunciation. In a highly acquisitive society, such as our own has increasingly become in the twentieth century, there is clear merit in arguing for a major reduction in consumerism and the desire for possessions. This is not quite the renunciation urged by Russell, which is perhaps not what most of us wish for, or could attain even if we did wish for it. But it is a significant step in that direction: one that brings considerable benefits by increasing peace of mind, and co-operation between individuals and whole societies.

All in all, the contemporary situation stands in need of improvement. The resurgence of religious influence, and the consequent hostility to or neglect of strict scientific method; the worsening of economic pressures on people with the growing emphasis on competitiveness; the international violence produced by both religious resurgence and the ruthless pursuit of economic interests on the part of the rich and the powerful: these are among the factors militating against the outlook which is truly appropriate to modern man, and which can offer genuine guidance, illumination and peace. Such is the outlook jointly provided by Russell and Santayana 100 years ago, and one that still awaits general adoption.

In conclusion, I'd like to add to what was previously said about the intellectual context in which Russell and Santayana wrote their seminal essays. Also, I'd like briefly to relate their outlooks to certain developments in twentieth-century Western literature.

On context: as part of the nineteenth-century heritage on which both philosophers drew, there is the work of the Italian poet Giacomo Leopardi. His poem *La Ginestra*, written as early in the century as 1836, remarkably foreshadows Russell and Santayana in its appeal for human unity amid a godless universe. Russell was directly influenced by Leopardi, and particularly by this poem, as he states in his *Autobiography*. His interest in the poet was shared by Santayana.

Another part of the inheritance is the work of the English novelist and poet Thomas Hardy, a leading literary figure of the later nineteenth century. Hardy's grim sense of cosmic process was much influenced, incidentally, by Schopenhauer, who in turn admired Leopardi. Also, there is a direct link between Leopardi's *La Ginestra* and a poem by Hardy called *A Plaint To Man*, which reasons that, in a godless universe, the only source of benevolence and solicitude toward man is man himself—is 'the human heart's resource alone/In brotherhood bonded close ...'

It should be added that the nineteenth-century heritage was not the only one to which Russell and Santayana turned. They also looked to the pre-Socratic Greek, particularly to Democritus. Both men, at various points in their work, praised the open-minded and rationalistic vigour of pre-Socratic ontological enquiry, establishing as it did the foundations of the scientific outlook in the West. As is well known, the pre-Socratics originated heliocentric, atomic and evolutionary theory, among other things.

Finally, on connections with developments in twentieth-century literature, the essential linkage is captured in the phrase 'the intensification of immanence'. If we define the immanent as the natural, as that which in principle is accessible to scientific investigation, then we see that the perspective articulated by Russell and Santayana is wholly immanent, as opposed to being supernaturalistic and transcendental. This same perspective became increasingly pronounced among many twentieth-century creative writers, who sought to intensify the experience of being inextricably located in a situation which was totally earth-bound and devoid of any transcendental dimension. The quest for intensity might be described as a humanistic inwardness: an exclusive concern with the texture of experience, a cleaving to the tangible, and a belief that the only 'spiritual' encounter possible is that which man has with himself and his fellow men.

The German poet Rainer Maria Rilke, for example, stressed the need to accept, indeed exult in, the transient and once-only character of human existence. A similar view is found in the French novelist Andre Gide. Another French novelist, Marcel Proust, dedicated himself to exploring the experience of remembering, regarding such exploration as possessing an absolute value. Further, the American poet Wallace Stevens saw the human imagination as something which should replace, as a basic source of sustenance, belief in deity. Many other twentieth-century writers, including Forster, Hemingway and the later Yeats, could be named as proponents of humanistic inwardness.

Their shared position can in fact be summed up in the words of Santayana. At one point in his work, he quotes a Spanish proverb: 'In order to rise high, one must sink deep.' There can be no question that, for Santayana and for Russell, the sphere to sink deep into is the human, no matter how fragile and impermanent the latter may be.

This point is the keynote of almost all the work which both philosophers subsequently produced in the twentieth century. Their outputs were of course enormous, with Santayana publishing almost until his death in 1952, and Russell almost until his death in 1970. Both ranged wide in the fields of ontology and epistemology, plus ethical, social and cultural philosophy. Also, Russell famously became deeply involved in some of the pivotal political issues of the twentieth century: protesting against World War One, and, after World War Two, against the nuclear arms race and US policy in Vietnam. He has come to be regarded by some as perhaps the greatest philosopher of the twentieth century. Santayana, though not quite as productive as Russell, nor politically active, steadily grew in reputation, chiefly in the period up to World War Two. In fact, during this period, A. N. Whitehead, Russell's associate, said that Santayana was the philosopher of his time most likely to be read in the future.

So, the scales of both men's achievements were huge. Yet, at their kernels, quietly speak the voices first heard in their essays of, respectively, 1900 and 1903: voices which assign absolute value to the human sphere, to its depth, reach and complexity, and to its strivings that find no echo, as far as present knowledge shows, in the cosmos lying beyond it.

Schopenhauer and Herman Melville

Though neither knew of the other's existence, the German philosopher (1788–1860) and the American novelist (1819–91) occupy significantly similar positions in nineteenth-century Western thought. This is especially so because of their pre-Darwinian location; by 1859, the year *The Origin of Species* was published, Schopenhauer had completed all his work,[1] and Melville had written his best novel. Though uninfluenced by Darwin, both achieved a view of the natural world which anticipated in striking fashion the Darwinian and neo-Darwinian perspectives that have been predominant in biology for the last 150 years.

Also, despite the tremendous density of sensuous detail characterising their respective views of nature, both asked questions about what reality might lie behind the physical world as apprehended by the sense faculties. Their thinking on this topic was not quite the same, but what is significant, and what marks them as men of the nineteenth century, is that the topic profoundly exercised them, in ways conditioned by the limitations in scientific knowledge to which their century was subject.

Finally, both thought that human evil was an ongoing reality; and both set great store by human genius, seeing it as the welcome antithesis of averageness and mediocrity.

Schopenhauer's picture of the natural world is linked to the fact that he was one of the first major Western philosophers since ancient times to be overtly atheistic. Hence he did not see the natural order as proof of the existence of a benevolent deity—or, indeed, of a deity of any kind. In this respect, he also departs from the perspective of most of the European Romantic poets of the early nineteenth century. His picture of nature was in fact a grim one; and, as said, it accords with the viewpoint of most biologists since Darwin. Of the struggle for existence, he writes:

> everywhere in nature we see contest, struggle and the fluctuation of victory ... This universal conflict is to be seen most clearly in the animal kingdom [which includes man]. Animals have the

[1] He was in fact to die a year later, in 1860.

> vegetable kingdom for their nourishment, and within the animal kingdom again, every animal is the prey and food of some other.[a]

Also:

> Junghahn [an explorer] relates that he saw in Java a plain, as far as the eye could reach, entirely covered with skeletons of large turtles ... which come this way out of the sea to lay their eggs, and are then attacked by wild dogs, who with their united strength lay them on their backs, strip off the small shell from the stomach, and devour them alive. But often then a tiger pounces on the dogs ... For this these turtles were born ... Thus the will to live everywhere preys upon itself, and in different forms is its own nourishment, till finally the human race, because it subdues all the others, regards nature as a manufactory for its own use.[b]

(Later, we will look at the term 'will to live' in some detail.)

Now, Melville, on the internecine character of marine life:

> Consider the subtleness of the sea; how its most dreaded creatures glide under water, unapparent for the most part, and treacherously hidden beneath the loveliest tints of azure. Consider also the devilish brilliance and beauty of many of its most remorseless tribes, as the dainty embellished shape of many species of sharks. Consider, once more, the universal cannibalism of the sea; all whose creatures prey upon each other, carrying on eternal war since the world began.[c]

But man, too, Melville adds, is a ruthless carnivore: 'Go to the meat market of a Saturday night and see the crowds of live bipeds staring up at the long rows of dead quadrupeds.'[d]

The sureness of Schopenhauer's and Melville's grasp of natural detail was, to repeat, supplemented by a concern with what might lie behind visible nature. Schopenhauer's approach to this question was stringently and systematically philosophical. He saw himself as heir to the transcendental idealism of Kant: namely, to the view that, while there is an external world existing independently of our mental and sense faculties, we can experience that world only in a subjectively transfigured way, as 'phenomena', but never know it directly, objectively, as 'noumenon'. Hence our knowledge of the natural world, however thorough, was only knowledge of phenomena, of reality as it appeared to us through the filters of our mental and sensory apparatus—not reality as it was separately from our modes of apprehending it. Objective reality was the noumenon.

What Schopenhauer postulated as noumenon was 'will'— something not, as we might think, of a psychological nature, but an entity which, as one Schopenhauer commentator has argued,[2] was akin to the 'energy' of modern physics: that is, a fundamental kind of force or power which was the universe's essential substance. Thus the natural world as we subjectively apprehended it in all its apparent variety was—objectively—nothing but this single, unitary will.

Schopenhauer emphasised the point that we could never have direct knowledge of the will. However, he went on to say that we could infer what the will was like from our subjective experience of it as phenomena; and because the phenomenal sphere, the world of nature which included all forms of life, was hideously chaotic,[3] we could validly deduce that the will was something blind, aimless and non-rational: a forever writhing, seething, tumultuous force, and nothing else. Of this force, the 'will to live', as referred to by Schopenhauer in the extract quoted earlier, was only phenomenal appearance: it belonged to the biological sphere, which was itself phenomenal, since the will, like the energy of modern physics, was at bottom sub-biotic.

In brief commentary on this position: if will is equated with the energy of physics, then Schopenhauer's views continue to be relevant, especially as the energy of physics is not apprehensible by the senses. However, energy is strictly a category in physics; and Schopenhauer, were he alive today, would probably argue that it was not the fundamental reality, precisely because it was a *scientific* category. He claimed that science could deal only with phenomena, not with the noumenon. Nevertheless, despite what we would now regard as its serious under-estimation of the scope of science, his perspective remains a poignant one, and certainly a remarkable achievement for his time: a time, we should remember, when Christian ontology was still predominant.

Unlike Schopenhauer, Melville did not work within a definite philosophical tradition, and was in any case a creative artist rather than a philosopher in any strict sense. His sources were culturally varied and eclectic—to an extreme degree, in fact. The question they collectively formed for him was this: was the fundamental reality a benign God or an inscrutable force which no form of theology could comprehend? Through the words of Captain Ahab in his greatest work, *Moby Dick*, Melville explores the following view:

---

[2] Bryan Magee, in *The Philosophy of Schopenhauer*, chapters 6 and 7.

[3] In the sense, not of being causeless, but of lacking moral structure or justification.

> All visible objects ... are but as pasteboard masks. But in each event—in the living act, the undoubted deed—there, some unknown but still reasoning thing puts forth the mouldings of its features from behind the unreasoning mask. If man will strike, strike through the mask!

Also, Ahab's relentless pursuit of the whale Moby Dick, which bit off his leg, is driven by the conviction that the whale is the visible mask behind which the invisible 'still reasoning thing' exists. Further, this thing is malicious, but inscrutably so: Ahab cannot account for its malice. Yet his ignorance does not prevent him from hating it: 'That inscrutable thing is chiefly what I hate.'[e] So it is by killing the whale that Ahab hopes to 'strike through the mask' of visible things and penetrate to the reality behind them.

The parallel with Schopenhauer will be clear: we again have a distinction between what can be grasped by the senses and what cannot—in Schopenhauerian terms,a divide between phenomena and noumenon. However, the difference is also evident: for Schopenhauer, the noumenon was blind and purposeless, whereas for Melville's Ahab, it was rational, and intentionally malevolent.

In contrast to Schopenhauer's postulate, Melville's has no linkage to modern science. Yet, like Schopenhauer's, it is arresting, dramatically and imaginatively, as a construction put on the massive violence of the natural world which both men saw so clearly. Its value lies less in itself than in the perceptions which gave rise to it. And again like Schopenhauer's, it constitutes a bold departure from the Christian orthodoxy of its day.

Moving now to the subject of human evil, the views of both writers ran parallel. They both regarded certain kinds of human viciousness as innate. Melville, in his novella *Billy Budd*, speaks of 'a depravity according to nature', while Schopenhauer avers that 'the wicked man is born with his wickedness as the snake is born with its poison fangs and its sack of venom, and the one can as little change his nature as the other.'[f] These claims, while applying to only a small number of malefactors, are ones which experience requires us to accept as valid. Experience indicates that the environmentalist explanation of vicious behaviour is not always correct.

Lastly, at the opposite pole from their reaction to the horrors of the natural world and of certain human beings, both men greatly valued genius. The panoramic perspective of the outstanding mind and sensibility was, for them, a source of inspiration and consolation in the face of what they saw as the general monotony of the human species. Schopenhauer's description of most people as 'Fabrikwaaren der Natur' ('Nature's manufactured articles') is famous. It is echoed by Melville's characterisation of mankind as 'a mob of unnecessary duplicates'.[g] By contrast, reverence for the exception is shown by Melville when he speaks of 'intellectual superiority' and the 'imperial brain',[h] and by his inscribing *Moby Dick* to fellow novelist Nathaniel Hawthorne, 'In Token of My Admiration For His Genius'. Schopenhauer, among the many things he said on the topic, wrote: 'Great minds, of which there is scarcely one in a hundred millions, are thus the lighthouses of humanity; and without them mankind would lose itself in a boundless sea of monstrous error and bewilderment.'[i]

That both men set such a high value on genius is perhaps an indicator of the revulsion they felt for, at the other end of the natural spectrum, the brute forces of nature. Certainly when reading them—especially Schopenhauer—one comes to a new appreciation of the large degree to which the exceptional person diverges from the sub-human order (and, as well, of the lesser degree to which the average person does). This view of mankind as, to varying extent, a departure from the rest of nature (though of course never a total departure), is now a commonplace of evolutionary biology. What sub-human nature consists of is conveyed by Schopenhauer and Melville with a vividness probably unequalled by any Western writers of the nineteenth century except biologists and philosophers of evolution (Darwin, Wallace, Huxley, Spencer). This graphicness adds even more force to what they say about those few human beings who stand at the maximal distance from the sub-human.

Endnotes

[a] *The World as Will and Representation*, vol. 1, tr. E. F. J. Payne (New York: Dover Publications Inc., 1958) pp. 146–7.

[b] As quoted by Will Durant, *The Story of Philosophy*, p. 285.

[c] Herman Melville, *Moby Dick* (Penguin Books edn. 1992[1851], chapter 57.

[d] *Ibid.*, chapter 65.

[e] *Ibid.* All quotations in this section are from chapter 36.

[f] As quoted by Patrick Gardiner in *Schopenhauer* (Harmondsworth: Penguin Books, 1963) p. 262.

[g] *Moby Dick*, chapter 107.

[h] *Ibid*, chapter 33.

[i] From the essay 'On genius' in *The Essential Schopenhauer* (London: Unwin Books, 1962) p. 74.

Comte's Continuing Relevance

Auguste Comte was born in 1798 and died in 1857. Though much in his writings is now dated, he remains a seminal figure in a number of respects. Firstly, he defined, as clearly as anyone has in the last 200 years, the pivotal and transformational role of science in the modern world. Next, despite this emphasis on the crucial importance of science, he rightly insisted that the purposes for which we utilise science can never be derived from science itself. That is to say, those purposes are affective and pre-rational in character. Thirdly, as a related point, he made an important contribution to the theory that human behaviour displays certain perennial and universal features, and that, in this sense, there is a human nature. Finally, as someone who regarded the supernaturalistic doctrines of religion as doomed, to be replaced by science, he advocated a particular form of humanism which many people find both realistic and satisfying.

However, before going on to look at these topics in some detail, let us, in the interests of balance, briefly say more about those aspects of Comte's work which are now outmoded. To begin with, he shared with Durkheim and Herbert Spencer a far too optimistic view of industrial capitalism, and wrongly assumed that this system, in contrast to feudalism, tended toward peace rather than war. Here, Marx, with his acute sense of the sectional and class interests at work in capitalism, was much more insightful about the system's capacity for conflict and aggression.[1] It was not that Comte failed to perceive class interests. In fact, he openly acknowledged that the capitalist system was and always would be controlled by those who were the wealthiest and most powerful. But he thought that this ruling class could be induced to exercise its power in ways which materially benefitted the whole of society as well as itself, thereby creating a harmony of economic interests.

As to how the ruling class could be so induced, Comte argued that the agency could and should be groups of scientists and philosophers: people of intellectual profundity and high moral calibre, who were also economically disinterested. They would constitute a kind

[1] A capacity on full display, of course, in the twentieth century.

of spiritual and moral order whose function would be to temper and limit the power of those who headed the economic order, and to give the latter moral guidance. However, once again, Comte can be charged with a gross lack of realism. As Marx and others would have asked: how exactly is the spiritual order to affect the economic? What effective power could the spiritual order impose on the economic if the latter simply refused to listen? These are questions perhaps too obvious to need stating, and ones rendered inevitable by the harsh experience of economic/political power since Comte's day; yet they are ones which Comte himself overlooked.

The criticisms which can be made of Comte on this score do not necessarily mean that all notions of a spiritual and moral sphere which is distinct from the economic are invalid. As we have seen, Durkheim had a number of interesting ideas on the same subject.[2] But it is clear that cogent thinking on this subject must include considerations of political and executive power. When it does, such thinking can be very significant indeed.

As regards Comte's views on science: while he rightly saw scientific development as the distinctive characteristic of the modern world, his overall view of science was, by contemporary standards, limited. For him, science was not an endless exploration of reality, an activity in which positions and perspectives were constantly being qualified, modified or amended. It was, on the contrary, a source of fixed and final certainties—indeed of dogma. In this, his viewpoint, with its classically Newtonian conception of scientific law as invariable, is emphatically pre-twentieth century.

Further, his conception of law in science was linked to one of law in history. Like Marx, though in a different frame of reference, he contended that there were laws of historical development; hence, that history travelled inexorably in a certain direction. Comte's frame of reference was one we shall soon examine in more detail: namely, an historical process by which mankind moved inevitably and totally from theological and metaphysical modes of thinking to one that was scientific and—because based on observation and direct experience—positivistic.

Comte's contention, asserting as it does the inevitable, complete and permanent triumph of the scientific over the non-scientific mind-set, is clearly at variance with many anti-scientific tendencies in the contemporary world, especially the resurgence of religious

[2] As did Comte's nineteenth- century contemporaries in England: Coleridge, Carlyle and Arnold.

fundamentalism and the continuing adherence to religion of a very large proportion of the world's population. The ultimate and global victory of the scientific outlook which Comte envisaged is, 150 years after his death, nowhere in sight: there are no indications of the historical inevitability of that triumph.

However, let us treat this point of criticism as a bridge to lead us back to positive commentary on Comte. We said at the beginning that he correctly identified the vital role of science in the modern world. As applied to the process of intellectual emancipation in Western Europe and North America in the nineteenth and twentieth centuries, Comte's point remains largely valid; likewise, as applied to the process of emancipation in other parts of the world. Science has unquestionably been the distinctive (though not only) agent of progress in the West and elsewhere over the last two centuries. This point needs of course to be qualified by the consideration that the effect of science on thought has been highly variable and remains so: that its influence on people has differed markedly in degree, depending on intellectual capacity, culture and environment. But even so, there can be no denying the fundamental changes it has produced. These changes make the intellectual history of the West since about 1800 qualitatively different from all preceding periods (though less so from the period 1700–1800 than from earlier centuries): a point which remains valid despite the persistence of various anti-scientific tendencies (as previously referred to).

Hence Comte was absolutely correct to draw a distinction between the predominantly scientific character of modern industrial society and the predominantly non-scientific character of pre-industrial, feudal society. In addition, he saw clearly that the scientist was largely replacing the ecclesiastic as society's source of ontological illumination (and now, at last, the illumination was genuine). Because, now, we do not normally look to religious bodies for factual instruction, we tend to forget that to do so was actually the norm in pre-scientific eras. Of this foundational change, we are forcefully reminded by reading Comte.

Let us now look in more detail at Comte's view of the intellectual history of mankind, a history which for him culminated in the attainment of the positivistic outlook. This history fell into three distinct phases. In the first, man tried to explain natural phenomena by attributing them to the actions of beings or forces like himself. This was the theological and animistic phase. In the second, phenomena were explained by reference, not to gods or spirits but to abstract entities such as 'nature'. This was the metaphysical phase. In the third and final phase, the one in which the most advanced minds were now located, man went no further than observing phenomena and perceiving regular links, laws, between them. He surrendered the notion, which had been characteristic of the theological and metaphysical stages, of a final principle or purpose lying behind observable facts, and was content to describe, in a purely empirical fashion, the workings of nature. This was the strictly scientific and positivistic phase.

Comte regarded the movement from one phase to another as inevitable because, as humanity's purview widened in thought and experience, the inadequacies of the theological and metaphysical viewpoints became increasingly obvious. Only the positivistic perspective could provide a full outlet for human enquiry. Hence positivism was man's ultimate intellectual destination—indeed, his destiny.

Comte's argument is clearly reasonable, and the three modes of thought he delineates are the chief three of which we have historical knowledge (although Comte's chronology of modes must be subjected to close historical and anthropological analysis). At the same time, we have to add to criticisms that were made earlier. Comte underestimated the power possessed by atavistic styles of thinking to stage come-backs—sometimes spectacular ones. Of this power, the aforementioned resurgence of religious fundamentalism is a recent example. In the West, that resurgence has been the most prominent in the United States, the country which also leads the world in science and technology. This shows that scientific advance provides no absolute guarantee against reversions to non-scientific or pre-scientific ways of thinking. A similar point can be made about Germany in the inter-war years: a country with a great scientific tradition which nevertheless succumbed to a primitive ideology. A further observation is that in many societies, science peacefully co-exists with religion of a non-fundamentalist, moderate and 'liberal' form. Overall, then, the picture is nowhere near as clear-cut as Comte thought. If it is true that mankind does move chronologically through the three intellectual stages, then this is the case only in a *partial* and *limited* sense. History shows no complete and irreversible transition from one phase to another. Hence there is no demonstrable law of total transition. The future is likely to evince, like past and present, a plurality of outlooks.

That said, what is of unquestionable importance for the secularist in Comte's outlook is his clear delineation of the positivistic mode of thinking. The movement from theology and metaphysics to positivism (including its more recent form, logical positivism) has essentially been a shift from a teleological to a mechanistic mode of explanation. In other words, positivism explains event-sequences only in terms of causal links between each event in the sequence, and not in terms of any pre-established purpose which the sequence as a whole is alleged to serve. Positivism embraces the concept of causal law, but does not equate law with purpose. Further, while Comte's notion of law was, as we have noted, Newtonian and too rigid, law is still of course a feature of scientific thinking; only now – as has been previously emphasised – it is seen not as invariable but as statistical and probabilistic.

In addition, positivism remains a key ontological approach despite the fact that it rests content with the notion of law, and does not seek metaphysical explanations for why laws are as they are. Elsewhere in this book, I have offered the view that seeking this kind of explanation is not to be dismissed as illegitimate; but that it is likely to be less profitable in achieving ontological clarity than the non-metaphysical approach.

Moreover, though it is true that the positivistic mind-set, associated as it is with empiricism and what is generally accepted as scientific method, is neither universal nor likely to become so in the foreseeable future, still the secularist cannot help wishing it *were so.* It deserves to be. Hence secularists can look for sustenance to Comte as being, in a general way, one of the great nineteenth-century advocates of science: albeit an advocate who, like several of his contemporaries, displayed an excess of rationalistic optimism in assuming that the scientific outlook would completely command the stage in mankind's future. If the scientific outlook were truly global, then all ideological conflicts based on ontological claims that are unverifiable or unfalsifiable would, quite simply, cease.

Comte's advocacy of positivism, for all its intensity, confined itself strictly to the task of describing the world. He did not, like Durkheim, see science as prescriptive as well as descriptive. In other words, he did not think that scientific knowledge could itself give us reasons for doing science. Reasons and motives for action were matters of ethics, not science, and were based on feelings, emotions, predilections. This distinction between the content of scientific activity and the reasons for performing such activity, plus the view that these reasons are affective, place Comte firmly in a tradition which can broadly be described as Humean. This tradition began with Hume in sharply distinguishing between facts and values, and in insisting that the latter cannot be derived from the former. For people in this tradition, scientific activity is undertaken to satisfy various emotional imperatives—not least the sheer desire or need for truth.

The emotivist theory of ethics, which remains a highly cogent one, led Comte to aver that one of the most important ethical and social tasks was to widen the range of unselfish and altruistic feeling. Since people acted, fundamentally, on the strength of their emotions, the route to social harmony and well-being was to increase the scope of those emotions which made for unity and mutuality.[3] This approach has obvious links with religion, particularly Christianity, at its rare best; but of course for Comte the perspective was humanistic; and all circumspect humanists will surely concur with it.

Comte's Durkheimian stress on the need for social harmony is bound up with his view of the fundamental oneness of the human race: a unity which was evident throughout history. This oneness consisted, firstly, in the primacy of emotion in the formation of motives for action; secondly, in man's constant need to act, to make his mark on the world around him; and thirdly, in his use of intelligence to act effectively, and so satisfy the emotions which underpinned his motives.

On the basis of this rather elementary picture of a permanent human nature, Comte builds a number of more complex and interesting arguments, in which he categorises different kinds of egoistic and altruistic feelings, plus different kinds of intellectual activity and willing. He claims that these various forms of emotion, thought and volition are permanent features of human behaviour, though they manifest themselves in various ways throughout history, according to the outlets and constraints of particular environments and milieux.[4]

---

[3] It is important to point out that Comte, like Durkheim but unlike Marx, did not think that violence was the solution to social and political problems. Solutions lay in changes of outlook and states of mind.

[4] Hence, for Comte, the study of history and social context remained very important. This could hardly have been otherwise for someone who was, after all, one of the founders of sociology. In fact, Comte made a leading contribution to the nineteenth-century's ground-breaking work in historical and contextualist thinking. Also, Comte's distinction between behavioural tendencies which were trans-historical, and particular

This contention that there exists a fixed human essence, has found parallels in subsequent thought, and is to be taken seriously. Reference has already been made to Pareto. Other names which could be mentioned are Santayana, Eliot, Freud and Jung. As long as we bear in mind the evolutionary perspective, and confine ourselves to humanity's present state of physical evolution and what we know of its capacities, there is indeed a case for arguing for recurring tendencies.

Finally, let us look at Comte's concept of a sociocracy. Like Durkheim, Comte recognised the individual's need to attach himself to something greater than himself, and saw that supernaturalistic outlooks could no longer meet this need. As a humanist, he argued that attachment could only legitimately be to something natural: namely, to the greatest human achievements in thought and action throughout the ages. Those individuals who had scaled the moral and cultural heights constituted a sociocracy, or, put another way, a social aristocracy—what we would now call a meritocracy. It was to this group that the rest of us should turn for guidance, sustenance, inspiration. Exceptional people transcended the human average, though not of course the human species, not humanity as a whole. Clearly, there is an overlap in Comte's thinking between the idea of sociocracy and that of a spiritual and moral hierarchy of human beings.

Comte's notion of sociocracy makes him, in effect, an aristocratic humanist, someone with—to borrow Nietzschean terms—a vertical rather than a horizontal perspective. This perspective has a strong appeal for all humanists who insist on discriminating between exception and average, and who therefore reject the extreme form of democratic thinking which does not acknowledge this distinction. There is a very powerful argument indeed for maintaining a sense of meritocratic hierarchy among human beings;[5] and those who, in the present and the future, continue to espouse it will find lasting support in Comte.

---

manifestations of those tendencies which were located in specific historical moments, has affinities with Vilfredo Pareto's theory of residues and derivations.

[5] An argument nowhere better stated, incidentally, than in Ulysses's speech on status, reputation and order in Shakespeare's *Troilus and Cressida.*

Max Weber

Widely regarded as the greatest modern sociologist—certainly as the greatest German sociologist since Marx—Weber (1864–1920) covered an encyclopaedic range of topics. Perhaps of chief interest to secularists are: (1) His exploration of religious culture, which was part of a project to enter sympathetically into the ethical outlooks and world-views of past societies, and so increase our imaginative understanding of the beliefs which sustained those societies. In this sensitive approach to the study of religion, he echoes Durkheim and Santayana. (2) His view that an absolute divide exists between facts and values, and that, therefore, the latter have to be chosen by an act of decision and will. There is no question of our factually *discovering* which values are right to choose. His keen sense of the difficulty of ethical choice prefigures Sartrean existentialism. (3) His conception of science as an ongoing, indeed never-ending activity, in which positions are constantly being qualified, modified, amended or even abandoned. Hence, he differs radically from Comte, and anticipates twentieth-century philosophers of science such as Popper. (4) In connection with his views on science, his awareness of the problems created by science's demystification of the natural world, its reduction of natural processes to ones which are useful to man but in themselves meaningless and without any sacred significance. Here, he foreshadows, among others, Heidegger, and harks back to the perplexities of the Romantic poets of the early nineteenth century. (5) His grasp of the enormous complexity of the social fabric: the inter-dependence of, and reciprocal interaction between, society's many elements and components, without any one single component's being primary or ultimate as a causal factor. This pluralistic outlook is as needed today as it ever was, given the persistence of monolithic and reductionist versions of social causation. (6) His concern for the integrity of the individual in the face of the increasing bureaucratisation of modern life: the widening threat to personhood of the growth of vast, anonymous organisations, both economic and political. This concern again links with existentialism. Also, Weber's interest in the individual led him to insist that particular people play a crucial role in history, over and above that played by general tendencies of a social and economic character.

Weber's studies of religious culture were wide-ranging. He examined Judaism, Hinduism and Buddhism, Taoism and Confucianism. However, his best known work in this field is on Christianity, or rather on one aspect of Christianity: *The Protestant Ethic and the Spirit of Capitalism*. In fact, this book does not even deal with the whole of Protestantism, but focuses on Calvinism. Weber argued that the growth of capitalism in North Western Europe was partly due to Calvinist ideas about a connection between the notion of personal salvation and a certain kind of economic activity. Without exploring the thesis in detail, it is sufficient to say that his reasoning goes against orthodox Marxism by contending that ideas and states of consciousness can contribute to the shaping of an economic system and way of life. Marxist orthodoxy, by contrast, argues that economic systems are always the ultimate—most decisive—causes of ideas and states of consciousness: so, never ultimately effects of the latter. According to Weber, however, the economic system of capitalism was partly an effect of a set of ideas, that of Calvinism.

Weber's thesis reflects his intense interest in past societies, their ways of thinking and their value-systems. Also, it evidences his enormous historical erudition: he has been described as the last of the major sociologists with an encyclopaedic knowledge of world history. This panoramic sense of the human past in all its cultural and psychological variety is vital to humanism and secularism.[1] In addition, his argument powerfully exemplifies his general view that social formations never have a primary or ultimate determinant: Calvinism was seen by Weber as, to repeat, only one cause of capitalism: there were other causes as well.

While deeply interested in religious culture, Weber nevertheless stood back from all religions and saw moral values, not as objects of divinely-instigated revelation, but as products of human choice and decision. They were chosen; not deduced from facts, and therefore not from science. Weber is, then, part of the post-Humean tradition of moral subjectivism and non-cognitivism. In this respect, he is like Comte but unlike Durkheim. However, more so than Comte, he perceived the problems in having to decide on values with no scientific, let alone theological or metaphysical, guidance for support. His work conveys the anxiety and drama of choice in ways which anticipate Sartre (as said) and the whole field of atheistic existentialism.

---

[1] As is attested by, for example, one of British secularism's greatest living figures, Harold Blackham. See in particular Blackham's *The Future of Our Past*.

His perception of difficulty was heightened by an awareness of the problem of conflict between different value-systems, as held by different groups, societies, cultures; and of the impossibility of resolving the conflict by appealing to purely objective criteria. For Weber, as for every secularist, no such criteria existed: all was relative, all contingent. To speak figuratively, the gods of Olympus were in conflict, and even Zeus could not be objective arbiter. Weber's meditations on this topic parallel those of Isaiah Berlin.[2]

Though mankind could not look to science for moral guidance, still science held for Weber a central place in the human adventure, as the region of ontological questing. It was a region, however, without boundaries, and humanity would have to accept this. The labour and toil would be endless, with no completion or final stage reachable. In particular, no certain knowledge of the future was possible. The pertinence of this view to contemporary perspectives in science, chiefly physics, is clear. Also, it is interesting to note that Weber's view of causality was probabilistic only: a position which accords with the modern concept of natural law as, to repeat, statistical, not invariable.

Even if the scientific project was, by its nature, incompletable, still science had done enough thus far to banish forever, for its adherents, the mythopoeic, magical, enchanted and sacred view of the natural world held by almost all pre-scientific cultures. Weber had unflinching insight into the psychological difficulties created by the sense of nature as a totally neutral, impersonal dimension, one that could be controlled and exploited, but one that was no longer a friend, equivalent or even superior to man.[3] (The transition from the latter view to the former is of course what Comte refers to when he speaks of the movement to positivism and a strictly scientific outlook.) For Weber, man could no longer project himself outward onto the natural world, and so identify with it. From this inability came a sense of cosmic homelessness. As said, these difficulties were explored by the Romantic poets before Weber, and by Heidegger and others after him.[4] The difficulties of course remain.

The problem of inability to identify with the natural world was, for Weber, matched by one of equal magnitude: the danger of the

---

[2] Further, the theme of moral conflict, it hardly needs to be said, is perennially central to great literature, especially drama.

[3] The notion of nature as a superior is found, for example, in Wordsworth's view that receptivity to nature can be a source of moral education for man.

[4] These others include, again, existentialists, with whom Heidegger can be broadly associated.

individual's being submerged in the man-made world of huge, impersonal and bureaucratic organisations. Weber saw large-scale organisation and bureaucratisation as in fact the distinctive feature of modern life (whereas Durkheim, conversely, had seen that distinctive feature as differentiation between individuals). In regarding mass-organisation as the fundamental tendency, Weber feared that the individual sphere would be irremediably damaged and stunted. In this respect, he shows himself to be a classical liberal. (His writings on this subject remind one strongly of, for example, those of Bertrand Russell.) They also strike, again, an existentialist note: the protest against society's 'pigeon-holing' of the individual, a protest which is so prominent a feature of existentialist thought, secular and religious.

Weber's anxieties grew out of his experience of capitalist society, and it is clear that this form of society, in its industrial, commercial and other structures, has indeed moved in a direction to justify those anxieties. At the same time, Weber thought that a socialist kind of society, were it to emerge, would also subordinate the individual to large, anonymous institutions: again, because this tendency was endemic to modern times. Indeed, Weber feared that, under socialism, the subordination of the individual would be even more severe. On this point, it is worth noting that his death in 1920 came only three years after the establishment of the USSR. While the latter's regime would not now be generally regarded as having been socialist, 'socialist' is what it called itself; and, had Weber lived, he would have undoubtedly found confirmation of his worst fears in the spectacle of Stalinism in the Soviet Union. A similar point could be made about Chinese 'socialism' after 1949.

One aspect of Weber's misgivings regarding the individual and mass-institutions was that, the more tightly organised and bureaucratised society became, the more fixed and rigidly demarcated became the individual's occupational role. This is actually a long-standing issue in sociology, bound up with the fact of extreme division of labour in the modern world, and one which deeply exercised Marx in the nineteenth century. However, whereas Marx saw the problem only in the context of capitalism, Weber, as we have noted, viewed matters in the context of modernity as a whole.

The restriction of the role of the individual, in occupational thought and action, was all the more problematic in that he could not look beyond the man-made sphere to the natural world as an area with which to identify. Nevertheless, there was, in Weber's eyes, a form of liberation—at least mental liberation—available, and this was political: giving support to outstanding people who were charismatic political leaders and who transcended the constrained circumstances under which most people lived. This giving of support was for Weber an inviolable right for the individual to exercise; it constituted a freedom otherwise denied by his conditions of daily life.

Weber's interest in charismatic leaders as figures who offer society something extraordinary, as a welcome contrast to the commonplace, banal and bureaucratic, is connected with his view of the importance in history of outstanding individuals. While recognising the significance of large-scale impersonal forces and 'massive facts' – social, economic, cultural – he nevertheless regarded these factors as always leaving a margin for individuals to take decisive action and so tip the scales. This area of individual input, combined with the play of arbitrary circumstances and accidents, meant that there were no laws of history which predetermined the course of events: no laws, therefore, the knowledge of which would bestow clairvoyance. In this, Weber again strongly reminds us of Russell, and also of the emphatic anti-historicism of Popper. Further, we recall that Weber's concept of causality was probabilistic only. Overall, his opposition to the notion of historical determinism is one which most contemporary secularists share.

Returning now to Weber's point about what exceptional leaders can offer modern society: while his argument clearly has merit, it is actually the only one in the group we have been examining which contains highly questionable implications. Its merit lies in its recognition of the value of the extraordinary, and in the distinction it draws between the exceptional and the mediocre. These evaluations are ones which modern society should certainly retain. On the other hand, there is obvious danger in a situation where enormous numbers of people look to certain individuals and their sphere of leadership activity, solely as an uplifting contrast to their own ways of life. If their own life-styles are hemmed in by mass-organisation and bureaucracy, then there is a strong possibility that they will transfer their enthusiasm and commitment almost entirely to those individuals who are not thus restricted, and so engage, in effect, in hero-worship. It scarcely needs saying that hero-worship is insidious for the worshippers and the worshipped. Had Weber lived longer, he would have witnessed in his own country what is probably the most monstrous example of this phenomenon in recorded history.

It is true that he regarded bureaucratisation as endemic, and so we can see why he viewed charismatic leadership as the only meaningful contrast to it. Also, we can sympathise with the frustrations felt by all those who work in highly bureaucratic organisations. But the question we must ask is: can bureaucracy and impersonality be radically reduced, given sustained effort? Many people will reply in the positive, and will indeed point to a number of developments in contemporary society where such reduction is actually being achieved. (See the earlier essay on Durkheim for some of these developments.) The larger the area for individual fulfilment, self-fashioning and creative co-operation with others, the smaller will be the need to look beyond one's own sphere of activity and experience to one that is remote, probably idealised, and seen virtually as a substitute for one's own context. Society should be of such a kind that no one is led to live at a heightened level by proxy; that level should be directly available to all. This position is surely at the heart of the liberalism with which Weber, at his best, can be identified.

To Weber's failure to perceive a wider range of ways in which modern society can develop must be added what many people would regard as another shortcoming: his intense nationalism. This nationalism may seem odd in the light of the fact that almost all the Weberian issues we have been examining are universally relevant to modern man, regardless of country. Yet Weber was a nationalist, despite his liberalism and generally complex ways of thinking. This was displayed in his contention that Germany should take its place among the world powers, since power was an expression of human greatness. Hindsight enables us to be critical of nationalism in all its forms, when viewed as a basis for acquiring power over other nations or for adopting a hostile stance toward them. That kind of perspective was a factor in the general European colonialism of the nineteenth century, and contributed to the outbreak of two world wars in the twentieth. It of course remains a problem in the twenty-first century.

However, these negative criticisms of Weber apart, let us briefly and finally return to those elements in his work which remain valid and contemporary. His imaginative and empathetic approach to the past, especially the religious past; his view of science as open-ended, and as having irreversibly transformed our cosmic outlook; his perspective on ethics as a field of difficult decision-making; his richly complex sense of what constitutes society; and his concern with the individual under threat from bureaucracy and impersonality: all these themes mark him as a key figure for secularists and for all panoramically-minded people of today.

The Non-Utopians of 1945

1945 was of course the year World War Two ended, with victory for the Allied powers—the USA, Britain, the Soviet Union and, marginally, France—over the Axis nations: Germany, Italy and Japan. This victory is seen as a turning-point in modern history, as the moment when the forces of fascism and imperialism were turned back by those of democracy and freedom.

There is a good deal of truth in this representation. Since 1945, neither Germany, Italy or Japan has reverted to fascism or imperialist expansion (even if dictatorship has continued to be a political reality in many other parts of the world). Also, the victorious nations, with the exception of the USSR, were and have remained ones in which governments are elected by universal suffrage, and in which there exists a very significant measure of freedom of speech and expression.

This said, however, a number of qualifications need to be made. In 1945, Britain and France were still the imperialist powers they had been previously and, though seriously weakened by war, they continued in that mode: Britain fought colonial wars in Malaya and Kenya, and France in Indo-China and Algeria. As regards the USA, it financially aided the French in Indo-China, and, after France's withdrawal, became the new Western presence in that region. This was part of a global American policy which has been widely defined as neo-colonialism, a successor to European colonialism, and which many see as currently being pursued in Iraq and Afghanistan.[1] Regarding the Soviet Union: it had not been politically democratic up to 1945, and would not begin to move towards democracy until its virtually expiring moments in the late 1980s. In the years immediately after 1945, it imposed its influence on the countries of eastern Europe, and went on to vie with the United States for global power.

These brief observations are a few among many of the same kind that could be made, but they perhaps suffice to indicate the complexities and ambiguities of the general political situation in 1945 and

[1] The literature on this subject is vast. One of the most eminent contributors to it is Noam Chomsky, whom I would recommend as the first to read.

afterwards. Matters were not, and never are, black and white; they were a very wide spectrum of shades of grey. Though the Allied nations defeated power-systems, they were themselves, though in a different way, power-systems. The domestic democratic procedure which three of them followed did not prevent their embarking on coercive foreign policies. In fact, the discrepancy between domestic and foreign policy becomes the more glaring, the more the latter is researched. In the case of the Soviet Union, there was very little discrepancy, coercion at home closely paralleling that abroad.

Though, as said, much more could be said on the tortuous character of the 1945 situation, I wish to narrow the focus to statements made in this year by just four writers: two of them famous, two not, but all displaying deep and clarifying insights. The writers are: Sir Karl Popper, Reinhold Niebuhr, Kingsley Martin and S. K. Ratcliffe. Their observations cover a range of subjects—social, ethical and cultural as well as political; in fact, their concerns are more of a general social kind than a specifically political one, and it is in this broader area that their commentary carries maximum weight.

In each case, the viewpoint is distinctly non-Utopian. This is a most important point, since there was, at a popular level, a surge of something like Utopianist thinking at the end of the war: a phenomenon quite understandable as a psychological reaction against the unprecedented horrors the war had unleashed. The widespread feeling was that things would not only get better—a realistic expectation—but that they would become incomparably better than they had ever been before. This was not a realistic expectation; partly because it ignored the fact that the pre-war power structures, economic and military, remained in place; but also partly because, those power structures aside, it was too generous in its prediction of the moral and intellectual performance of the majority of people in post-war society. The generosity was, again, understandable, given the psychological climate, but still erroneous.

Such lack of realism is definitely not a charge that can be levelled against the writers under discussion. Let us begin with Popper, and his renowned book of 1945, *The Open Society and its Enemies.* Here, he argues for piecemeal social reform rather than the sweeping, utopianist variety which had been attempted in the Soviet Union in the inter-war years (in accordance with that regime's prevailing ideology). Popper's argument in fact has even larger scope: it is directed against all social projects premised on what he saw as the false ideological assumption that perfect societies are possible. Poignantly,

Popper avers that efforts to create a heaven on earth produce only the opposite effect. With their doctrinal rigidity, they actually create new evils, adding to the ones which, he insists, are perennial and ineradicable. Better, then, he argues, to have moderate, limited objectives which are achievable, than vastly over-ambitious schemes which self-implode. The wisest course is to attack specific evils,[2] perversities and uglinesses, in the hope of eliminating some and reducing others. Further than this it is unadvisable to venture.

Popper's modest proposal is one which most reflective people now endorse. The heady expectations of 1945 are very much a thing of the past. A far less sanguine approach to social reform is today the norm.

Moving on to Niebuhr, a leading theologian of the twentieth century: he parallels Popper in a number of ways, chiefly in his conviction of the impossibility of perfect societies. His 1945 book, *The Children of Light and the Children of Darkness,* focuses on what he sees as the perennial problem of conflict between self-interest and altruism. The 'children of light' are the unselfish people who think that this conflict can be easily resolved; whereas the 'children of darkness' know this is not the case, precisely because they are the ones with selfish motives, and are aware how potent those motives are. The forces of darkness, says Niebuhr, quoting St. Luke, 'are, in their generation, wiser than the Children of Light'. They recurrently challenge, and may defeat, the altruistic project of creating a better world.

When discussing efforts to build a world community from the ruins of war, Niebuhr characterises this task as a 'perpetual problem', and says that those undertaking it must always be 'prepared for new corruptions on the level of world community which drive simpler idealists to despair'.[a] No-one with extensive experience of social and political issues over the last sixty years is likely to dispute Niebuhr's arguments. Selfishness, on both large and small scales, appears to be a permanent feature of human affairs.

Turning now to Kingsley Martin: in a public lecture[b] given in 1945, Martin passed a distinctly sober verdict on post-war reformist expectations by averring: 'we must face the fact that comparatively few people have a passion for truth as a principle, or care about public events continuously when these do not obviously affect their own lives'. That this is unfortunately true is a realisation which

[2] And one is bound to add that these should include oppressive power structures.

emerges from long experience; and here Martin concurs with a line of thinkers stretching back to the ancient Greeks. He goes on to say:

> The outlook is not, in 1945, propitious ... The upshot will not be any kind of Utopia, but a new phase of human society, both better and worse than the one before it, but in any case necessary, because men must adjust their society to their knowledge.

This view of society as a mixed picture, containing gains and losses, advances and setbacks, merits and demerits, is the essence of the non-Utopianist perspective, which sees neither progress nor regress as total and linear. Also non-Utopianist is the gritty spirit of resilience, adaptability and stoicism which Martin's words convey.

Finally, to S. K. Ratcliffe. Again the reference is to a 1945 public lecture.[c] Entitled 'The eclipse of liberalism', the talk deals with the difficulties which liberal thinking has always encountered in society, and gives special attention to the challenges presented to rationalist liberalism by contemporaneous cults of irrationalism in the arts and religion. Ratcliffe concludes by contending that genuine advances in freedom of thought 'can never be other than slow and imperfect. In order to escape disappointment and disillusion, our hopes of advance and fulfilment must be kept within modest limits.'

The common message, then, in all four writers is that the goals to be pursued, and the hopes to be entertained, should be limited, moderate and realistic. This of course is not a doctrine of defeat; it is constructive and progressive, but in a restrained and highly qualified way. Sixty years later, the accumulated total of public and private experience points ever more steadily to the truth of that message: one that these writers were of course not the first to deliver, but one which they distinguished themselves by delivering at a time when the popular imagination was, to a large extent, yielding to the recurrent temptation of unfettered hope.

Endnotes

[a] *The Children of the Light and the Children of the Darkness* (London: Nisbet and Co., 1945) p. 128.

[b] This was in fact a Conway Memorial Lecture, delivered at Conway Hall, Red Lion Square, London W.C.1. The text of the lecture, from which I quote, is available from the Library of the South Place Ethical Society at Conway Hall.

[c] This talk was also given at Conway Hall, though not as a Memorial Lecture but as a presentation to the South Place Ethical Society, of which Ratcliffe was a member. The text is again available from the S.P.E.S. Library, in the journal *The Monthly Record* for 1945.

Montesquieu's Multiplicity

Though an eighteenth-century thinker whose context was the society of France's *ancien régime,* Montesquieu is important to contemporary liberal humanism in a range of ways.

Firstly, like Durkheim, he advocated social heterogeneity and diversity, and—like Locke in the seventeenth century—saw a balance of power and influence between different social groups as the guarantor of liberty. Where such variety and balance existed, no one group could be dominant.

This position has obvious relevance to present-day society; and, taken broadly, is an effective riposte to both the political Right and to certain elements on the political Left. To the Right, it says that economic power should not be concentrated in the hands of a few; and, to elements on the Left, that no one social class, no matter how large, should exercise a dictatorship (even if temporary) over other groups. Also, it points out to these elements just how many groups there are in addition to the one allegedly deserving to exercise dictatorship, and to the one which is economically dominant.

Montesquieu's interest in heterogeneity and balance was bound up with a quintessentially liberal concern for the individual context. If no form of social power should be unlimited, then that included the power of the majority. Montesquieu perceived that popular sovereignty and the general will could undermine the liberty of the individual citizen. Such undermining has in fact been evident since his day, in extreme forms of democratic culture, and even in mass-endorsement of totalitarian regimes. His anxiety about the dangerous possibilities of the general will foreshadows that of Tocqueville and Mill in the nineteenth century, and of several liberal thinkers since.

His complex sense of the social structure was matched by a multi-faceted view of social causation. Here, he resembles Weber, and is pertinent to contemporary thinking in the same way Weber is: as providing a capacious and finely-tuned alternative to crudely reductionist perspectives in sociology. Montesquieu regarded social reality as an endless interaction of different factors, and as influenced by a spectrum of causes, each with its own particular status: climate, religion, cultural heritage, morals, customs, laws—*in addition to* economics. The totality of these factors produced what he called the 'spirit' of a nation, and nations manifestly differed in 'spirit'. This wide-ranging explanatory approach is unquestionably the one that is needed today, to nullify the narrow dogmatisms which still vitiate social thought, and which did so in the past with inhumane, totalitarian consequences. Only with this approach can the full intricacy of human institutions be understood.

Finally, bearing in mind the topic of the previous essay, Montesquieu was not utopianist in politics. He saw political change as an alternation of advances and setbacks—hence, as not displaying any continuous or linear progression. In this, subsequent history again supports him to a considerable extent, and makes him a major point of reference for those who do not idealise politics. Montesquieu was in all things a moderate, and that included the hopes he placed in political activity.

Do Humanists Need the Concept of Evil?

Humanists definitely need *a* concept of evil, as a logical supplement to what they largely have already: a concept of good or goods. However, the requisite notion of evil should be independent of concepts originating in non-humanistic schemes of thought (chiefly religions), and therefore autonomous of certain traditional ideas which the term '*the* concept of evil', as given in the essay title, might evoke. An appropriate concept of evil is required, then, to fill a crucial gap in an already existing general framework of morality (a framework which includes, importantly, engagement in moral speculation and debate).

Let's begin by making some elementary points about this general framework. No humanist will deny that moral anchorage in some form is indispensable for a humane, constructive, consistent and socially satisfying way of life. The rejection of religious belief clearly does not mean the spurning of morality and moral concerns. While these points are non-controversial, the issue for humanists is of course what kind of anchorage to choose, and on what grounds to choose it. For any conscientious humanist, choice must be autonomous and not heteronomous: it must be opted for independently of coercion and/or authority, because only then can it be rationally vindicated and justified.

The question of autonomy and rational justification is central, since most humanists are not moral realists/cognitivists/objectivists. In other words, they do not think moral values are objects of discovery and knowledge, i.e., things existing objectively in the world external to mental experience, and therefore things we can cognise, perceive and learn about. Hence, they stand in diametric opposition to many religious believers, who argue precisely the opposite: that values are indeed 'out there' in the world, existing independently of the human mind and awaiting discovery by it. This argument takes the form of asserting that moral values are objective realities because they are creations of deity. As such, they are external to the human mind and may therefore become objects of knowledge to the latter. A variant of this argument is that, as divine creations, they are implanted by deity in the human mind, so that the latter can discover them within itself. What is common to both arguments is the view that moral values are not creations of the human mind; and it is this position that most humanists deny.

Such denial is obviously bound up with the fact that humanism eschews the notion of deity and therefore of divinely created values. For humanists, values have to be human creations, and freely adopted, since—to repeat—only then can they be seen as autonomous and rationally defensible. If they were discoveries, the question of independence and rational argumentation would not arise: the discoverer plays no part in what has been discovered; he is simply observer, spectator to it, and acquiescent in it; he is passively dependent on it as fact. There is no requirement to rationally defend what has been brought to light; the latter is an indisputable given, so there is no issue of arguing for it. By contrast, moral values regarded as mental creations cry out to be argued for; they automatically require defending and vindicating. And this is an obligation which, challenging though it may be, every humanist should vigorously embrace.

It follows that, for humanists, advocacy is the only genuine form of philosophical discourse in ethics, since it is not grounded on knowledge-claims but is a matter of argumentation and effort to persuade. (Though advocacy may refer to knowledge-claims and facts, such reference is not its main component.) In this respect, Hume, with his pivotal contention that morality is based on feeling, not knowledge, remains a seminal figure in humanist discourse; indeed, he provides the basis for arguing that humanist discourse in ethics is essentially a dialectic between different affective or attitudinal positions. Further, all humanists should accept the fact that discourse is a highly complex and ongoing affair: an inescapable feature of what might be described as the humanist condition.

To recapitulate on the main points made so far: the mainstream humanist position in ethics is non-realist, non-cognitivist, non-objectivist. Its values are therefore created ones: ones it has formulated and made a conscious decision to adopt and argue for. So, what specifically are its values? We have already said that it possesses a concept of good or goods. This concept is complex and extensive, but suffice it to say for present purposes that an emphasis is placed on general well-being and flourishing. (Note, for example, the popularity of utilitarianism among humanists.) This emphasis, eudaemonistic in character, implies, among many other things, freedom of thought, enquiry and speech, plus opportunity for maximal self-development and fulfilment of capacity. A final general point about the humanist concept of good is that humanists seek, as far as possible, to universalise it, on the grounds that its adoption would maximise the flourishing of the species.

Since, then, humanism possesses the positive concept that a moral framework requires, it needs, as said, the concomitant negative concept. This, like its opposite number, must be created, chosen, autonomous and not heteronomous. It cannot legitimately be a received idea. This does not mean that it cannot parallel or at least bear similarities to a traditional and established notion of evil, but only that it cannot be a borrowing or claim the status of moral knowledge. Clearly, if it were a mere borrowing or a knowledge-claim, there would be no obligation to argue for it in its own right, or to advocate it.

What, then, might be the substance of a created concept of evil? Manifestly, most of its content would be the converse of that contained in the concept of good. Factors which threaten or reduce general well-being, intellectual freedom and self-development would be foremost amongst those called evil. Some of these factors might well be what religious believers also call by the same name, but again the difference is that most humanists, in passing their judgement, would never speak of moral discovery or knowledge.

Humanists might choose to define evil as a ruthlessly exclusive pursuit of self-interest, on the part of single individuals or of groups. Such a pursuit is clearly inimical to the positives given above, and to the overall democratic and humanitarian values which most humanists hold. Whether it is this or some related definition that is chosen, humanists need to be explicit and specific, so as to have a solid basis for moral censure and, where necessary, for legal action. (On the latter, more will be said later.)

However, even when a definition is established, there are still other points to consider. For those humanists—hopefully the majority—who have a scientific outlook, actions deemed evil must be considered in causal terms. This is so because the scientific project, at least at the macroscopic level of events, is a search for causes and causal regularity. Thus the scientific mode of explanation is causal in character. If, then, scientific humanism censures an evil action, it also seeks to understand its origins and antecedents, no matter how various they may be. The causalist perspective rejects the idea of absolute and unconditioned free-will, so its concept of evil differs radically from that of those religious doctrines which do believe in absolute free-will.

It perhaps goes without saying that to view an evil action as caused does not mean taking no measures against it. To explain an action is not to acquiesce in it. An action is no less objectionable or harmful because it has a cause.The scientific humanist should therefore support forceful measures taken against the evildoer – though, it should be added, chiefly for their intended reformative effects: the aim being to change for the better the malefactor's future motives and reasons for action.

A further consideration, also to do with causality, is connected with ideology. A number of the most appalling actions in human history have been carried out by men actuated by an ideology or belief-system of some kind (secular or religious). Thus motivated, these men thought their actions were right and just. They did not regard themselves as evil; they saw their cause as valid, at least partly irrespective of the fact that they, as individuals, adhered to it. In the twentieth century, Hitler was one example, Stalin another, and Pol Pot a third. Many more instances can of course be adduced. Now, casting our minds back to what was proposed earlier as an appropriate humanist definition of evil, we must assume that the Hitlers and Stalins would reject the charge of self-interest, in relation to themselves, their political organisations, their nation and so on.

In dealing with causal factors of an ideological nature, the concept of evil as excessive self-interest would have to be modified; and with reference to scientific criteria. The argument could run as follows: the only way of justifying destructive actions derived from ideology is by showing that the ideology is factually correct; that it constitutes a true description of reality. This does not mean that the proven correctness of an ideology automatically justifies destructive action in its name; only that it is the only possible and available source of such justification. So, a burden of proof lies on the ideology. If the ideology fails to provide proof (as, for example, those of Hitler, Stalin and Pol Pot failed to), and if the exponents of the ideology either know of this failure or neglect to check if failure has been demonstrated or at least considered, then their subsequent destructive actions may justly be described as evil, even if the latter are disinterested.

The above argument is obviously one which any intelligent and mentally balanced person would deploy, and it is one which accords the most closely with scientific humanism.

At a simpler psychological level, where causal factors are not, and not alleged to be, ideological and disinterested, then the self-interest argument can be straightforwardly applied. This is the case with, for example, the criminal who has no other motive than material gain for himself and his group.

It is also applicable at a more complex psychological level, in the case of motivation of the kind denoted by the German word *schadenfreude*: pleasure in inflicting pain and suffering on another person, for no other reason than this enjoyment. Here, self-interest is psychological rather than material, and, again, excessive and ruthlessly exclusive.

So, in conclusion: the concept of evil proposed in this essay would, if adopted, fill a major gap in humanist thinking. Also, its adoption would emphatically not be a concession to moral cognitivism or dogmatism. While holding the concept, humanists would never for a moment forget its status as a creation, and as one based on feeling. At the same time, they would see it as possessing an ongoing validity, in a wholly naturalistic sense: that is, as valid for as long as human beings remain what, on the whole if in varying degree, evolution has made them—mutually responsive, co-operative and, to use the traditional phrase, social animals.

Celebrating Human Complexity

If it is agreed that mankind is the most complex form of life known to us, then that complexity, as a product of evolution, should be the continual focus of our thinking. If it is also agreed that some people are more complex than others, and that not all kinds of complexity are prepossessing, then these two considerations serve to qualify, but not invalidate, that focus. Hence the general fact of complexity should be the object of meditation, with particular attention paid to the forms of it which are prepossessing and creative.

Much that is perverse and destructive in behaviour is bound up with failure to appreciate complexity, that of others and of self. This is obviously the case with the desire to dominate others, including the project of imposing conformity from fear of originality: from, that is, fear of the unfamiliar and the challenging. The point applies equally to the project of exploitation, especially economic, and to several other projects as well. It is an old saying that many of those who wish to command others do so because they have failed to achieve self-command: failed, therefore, to engage with their own inner complexity, and so are unable to engage with that of others.

Perception of complexity should lead to the harnessing of all the positive energies the latter contains. The effort should always be constructive, contributory, toward the attaining of uplifting outcomes.

Complexity inevitably involves psychological pain, as the price of the encounter, but the pain is mind-enlarging, expanding awareness according to degree of capacity for such expansion. What should be remembered is that this point about capacity for enlargement applies equally to the experience of joy. The complex is of course, by its very nature, multifarious. Further, even if painful insight amplifies to tragic vision, the latter should be seen as an achievement of mind, of the same mind that contains resources also for the rarest and subtlest kinds of edification and happiness. For example, the 'To be or not to be' soliloquy in *Hamlet*, and other key moments in Shakespeare's tragedies, came from the same cognitive depths which engendered his comedies and post-tragic plays. That depth we, the readers, can share.

Reference to Shakespeare points to the general topic of art's role in holding 'the mirror up to nature,' a nature of staggering plasticity and diversity. By common agreement, the greatest art is that which is fully commensurate with nature's magnitude and variety; or, as John Ruskin says, that which is 'capable of arousing the greatest number of the greatest ideas.'[1] Hence Shakespeare, Tolstoy, Goethe, Dickens, Proust, Homer, Dante and other great writers are rightly regarded as such because of the inclusiveness of their material, in addition to their artistic orchestration of it.

It is reasonable to suppose that their spanning of complexity induced in them moments of a purely contemplative savouring of the vastness they had encompassed: a kind of luminous stasis. Further, if a naturalistic evolutionary perspective is the one which a scientifically-minded humanity will increasingly adopt, then luminous stasis could be regarded as the ultimate attitude of the future. Man will of course continue to act, both on the environment and on himself, to change, prevent, improve, modify, amend. But the action, and the capacity for it, will increasingly be seen as themselves products of evolved physical intricacy; and the latter will more and more induce meditation, a sense of wonder, a desire for celebration. Moreover, as knowledge of this intricacy enlarges with the advance of science, the desire to celebrate the tangibly complex will replace the impulse, dominant in pre-scientific cultures and in mentalities insufficiently responsive to available science, to look to an alleged supernatural sphere as the supposed source of the tangible.

The science-nourished mankind of the future will perhaps find its greatest satisfaction in savouring the fact of being on a continuing evolutionary trajectory which has already carried humanity to its condition of biological uniqueness, and to the social, artistic and scientific achievements flowering from that singularity.

[1] As quoted by Raymond Williams in *Culture and Society, 1780-1950*, p. 143.

The Purposeful and the Purposeless

Human beings obviously have purposes. Less obvious, however, is the fact that these purposes are, in a very important respect, effects of processes which are purposeless. The latter processes are genetic. They can be seen as the primary causes of purposive action in that they are the source of the primal will-energy, the general vital momentum, impelling all the particular purposes which the individual, situated as he is within a specific environment, embarks on. In addition, they are the fount of all capacity for pursuing and attaining purposes: hence the condition for that pursuit and attainment.

We can in fact go even further, and say that genetic processes are not only general sources, in the ways described above, but also founts of certain particular purposes such as self-preservation and procreation: ones which are, biologically, absolutely basic, and therefore inevitable in all environments.

Genetic processes are driven by a causality which is mechanistic, not teleological. Hence, if we take the project of genetic engineering, purpose entails a harnessing of forces which are without purpose, for the achieving of eugenic objectives. This involves, in Bacon's famous phrase, obeying nature in order to command her; but the nature being obeyed is, as said, mechanistic; so it is a matter of the mechanistic being brought into the service of the purposive human agent—through the knowledge which the agent possesses of the mechanistic.

The agent is, of course, also a part of nature; but, to repeat, his purposiveness has a primary source in the purposeless. So, without purposeless areas in nature, purposeful ones could not exist. Also, as in eugenic projects, the latter rely on the former to reach their goals.

Science and Social Action

We could perhaps define the psychological need which supernaturalistic religious beliefs have traditionally sought to satisfy as the need to attain the most capacious, the most emotionally inclusive, mode of response to one's fellow human beings. This need is perennial; and, with the decline of supernaturalism, it must now be met in ways which (in contrast to supernaturalism) do not clash with the scientific perspective.

One route to achieving that deepest response-level is social and political involvement—provided the latter is free of anti-scientific ways of thinking. In fact, in a culture which is genuinely scientific, it is a main route, since it can share with science a complete independence of belief in the supernatural. Hence, once social co-operation has been chosen, science can nourish and reinforce that commitment, supplying, as science itself develops, an ever-expanding means to attain moral ends. In this way, science can be integral to the achievement of the profoundest mutuality and comradeship through social action.

Index of Names

Who Holds the Moral High Ground?

Colin J Beckley and Elspeth Waters

Meta-ethical attempts to define concepts such as 'goodness', 'right and wrong', 'ought' and 'ought not', have proved largely futile, even over-ambitious. Morality, it is argued, should therefore be directed primarily at the reduction of suffering, principally because the latter is more easily recognisable and accords with an objective view and requirements of the human condition. All traditional and contemporary perspectives are without suitable criteria for evaluating moral dilemmas and without such guidance we face the potent threat of sliding to a destructive moral nihilism. This book presents a possible set of defining characteristics for the foundation of moral evaluations, taking into consideration that the female gender may be better disposed to ethical leadership.

128 pp., £8.95/$17.90, 9781845401030 (pbk.), January 2008, *Societas,* Vol.32

Froude Today

John Coleman

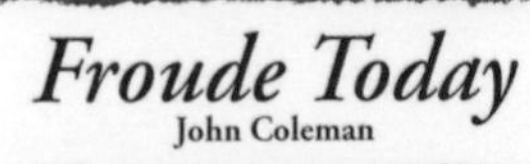

A.L. Rowse called fellow-historian James Anthony Froude the 'last great Victorian awaiting revival'. The question of power is the problem that perplexes every age: in his historical works Froude examined how it applied to the Tudor period, and defended Carlyle against the charge that he held the doctrine that 'Might is Right'.

Froude applied his analysis of power to the political classes of his own time and that is why his writings are just as relevant today. The historian and the prophet look into the inner meaning of events – and that is precisely what Froude did – and so are able to make judgments which apply to ages far beyond their own. The last chapters imagine what Froude would have said had he been here today.

96 pp., £8.95/$17.90, 9781845401047 (pbk.), March 2008, *Societas,* Vol.33

Imprint Academic, PO Box 200, Exeter EX5 5HY, UK
Tel: +44(0)1392 851550. Email: sandra@imprint.co.uk

The Enemies of Progress

Austin Williams

This polemical book examines the concept of sustainability and presents a critical exploration of its all-pervasive influence on society, arguing that sustainability, manifested in several guises, represents a pernicious and corrosive doctrine that has survived primarily because there seems to be no alternative to its canon: in effect, its bi-partisan appeal has depressed critical engagement and neutered politics.

It is a malign philosophy of misanthropy, low aspirations and restraint. This book argues for a destruction of the mantra of sustainability, removing its unthinking status as orthodoxy, and for the reinstatement of the notions of development, progress, experimentation and ambition in its place.

Al Gore insists that the 'debate is over'. Here the auhtor retorts that it is imperative to argue against the moralizing of politics.

Austin Williams tutors at the Royal College of Art and Bartlett School of Architecture.

96 pp., £8.95/$17.90, 9781845400989 (pbk.), May 2008, *Societas,* Vol.34

Forgiveness: How Religion Endangers Morality

R.A. Sharpe

In his book *The Moral Case against Religious Belief* (1997), the author argued that some important virtues cease to be virtues at all when set in a religious context, and that, consequently, a religious life is, in many respects, not a good life to lead. In this sequel, his tone is less generous to believers than hitherto, because 'the intervening decade has brought home to us the terrible results of religious conviction'.

R.A. Sharpe was Professor Emeritus at St David's College, Lampeter. The manuscript of *Forgiveness* was prepared for publication by his widow, the philosopher Lynne Sharpe.

128 pp., £8.95 / $17.90, 9781845400835 (pbk.), July 2008, (*Societas* edition), Vol.35

To qualify for the reduced (subscription) price of £5/$10 for current and future volumes (£2.50/$5.00 for back volumes), please use the enclosed direct debit form or order via imprint-academic.com/societas

Healing, Hype or Harm? Scientists Investigate Complementary or Alternative Medicine

Edzard Ernst (ed.)

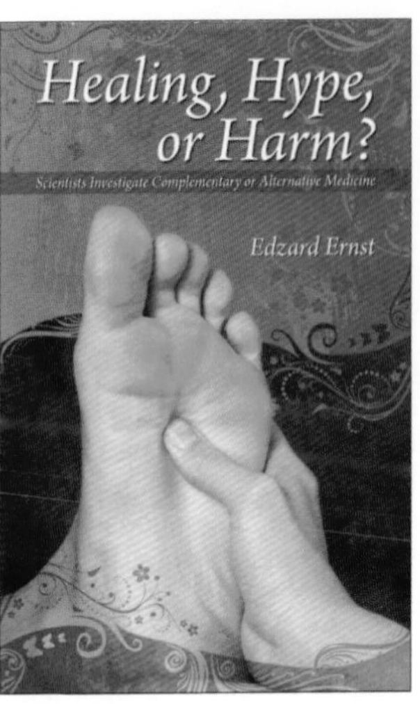

The scientists writing this book are not 'against' complementary or alternative medicine (CAM), but they are very much 'for' evidence-based medicine and single standards. They aim to counter-balance the many uncritical books on CAM and to stimulate intelligent, well-informed public debate.

TOPICS INCLUDE: What is CAM? Why is it so popular? Patient choice; Reclaiming compassion; Teaching CAM at university; Research on CAM; CAM in court; Ethics and CAM; Politics and CAM; Homeopathy in context; Concepts of holism in medicine; Placebo, deceit and CAM; Healing but not curing; CAM and the media.

Edzard Ernst is Professor of Complementary Medicine, Universities of Exeter and Plymouth.

190 pp., £8.95/$17.90, 9781845401184 (pbk.), Sept. 2008, *Societas,* Vol.36

The Balancing Act: National Identity and Sovereignty for Britain in Europe

Atsuko Ichijo

This is a careful examination of the historical formation of Britain and of key moments in its relations with the European powers. The author looks at the governing discourses of politicians, the mass media, and the British people.

The rhetoric of sovereignty among political elites and the population at large is found to conceive of Britain's engagement with Europe as a zero-sum game. A second theme is the power of geographical images – island Britain – in feeding the idea of the British nation as by nature separate and autonomous. It follows that the EU is seen as 'other' and involvement in European decision-making tends to be viewed in terms of threat. This is naive, as nation-states are not autonomous, economically, militarily or politically. Only pooling sovereignty can maximize their national interests.

Atsuko Ichijo is Senior Researcher in European Studies at Kingston University.

150 pp., £8.95/$17.90, 9781845401153 (pbk.), Nov. 2008, *Societas,* Vol.37

Seeking Meaning and Making Sense

John Haldane

Here is an engaging collection of short essays that range across philosophy, politics, general culture, morality, science, religion and art.

The author contributes regularly to *The Scotsman* and a number of radio programmes. Many of these essays began life in this way, and retain their direct fresh style.

The focus is on questions of Meaning, Value and Understanding. Topics include: Making sense of religion, Making sense of society, Making sense of evil, Making sense of art and science, Making sense of nature.

John Haldane is Professor of Philosophy and Director of the Centre for Ethics, Philosophy and Public Affairs in the University of St Andrews.

128 pp., £8.95/$17.90, 9781845401221 (pbk.), Jan. 2009, *Societas,* Vol.38

Independent: The Rise of the Non-aligned Politician

Richard Berry

Martin Bell, Ken Livingstone and Richard Taylor (the doctor who became an MP to save his local hospital) are the best known of a growing band of British politicians making their mark outside the traditional party system.

Some (like Livingstone) have emerged from within the old political system that let them down, others (Bell, Taylor) have come into politics from outside in response to a crisis of some kind, often in defence of a perceived threat to their local town or district.

Richard Berry traces this development by case studies and interviews to test the theory that these are not isolated cases, but part of a permanent trend in British politics, a shift away from the party system in favour of independent non-aligned representatives of the people.

Richard Berry is a political and policy researcher and writer.

128 pp., £8.95/$17.90, 9781845401283 (pbk.), March 2009, *Societas,* Vol.39

Progressive Secular Society and other essays relevant to secularism

Tom Rubens

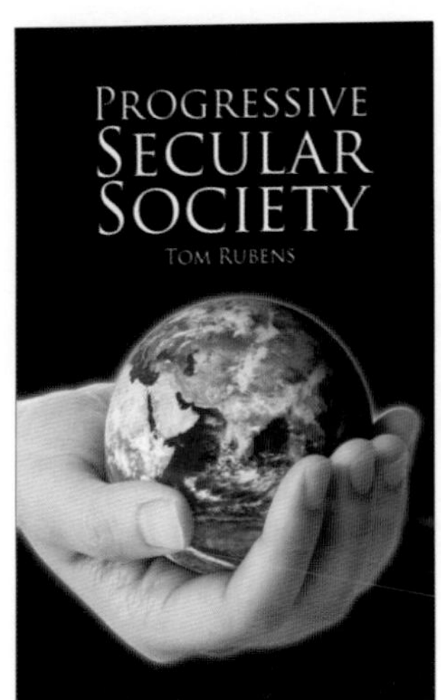

A progressive secular society is one committed to the widening of scientific knowledge and humane feeling. It regards humanity as part of physical nature and opposes any appeal to supernatural agencies or explanations. In particular, human moral perspectives are human creations and the only basis for ethics.

Secular values need re-affirming in the face of the resurgence of aggressive supernatural religious doctrines and practices. This book gives a set of 'secular thoughts for the day' – many only a page or two long – on topics as varied as Shakespeare and Comte, economics, science and social action.

Tom Rubens teaches in the humanities at secondary and tertiary levels.

128 pp., £8.95/$17.90, 9781845401320 (pbk.), May 2009, *Societas,* Vol.40

Self and Society (enlarged second edition)

William Irwin Thompson

The book contains a series of essays on the evolution of culture, dealing with topics including the city and consciousness, evolution of the afterlife, literary and mathematical archetypes, machine consciousness and the implications of 9/11 and the invasion of Iraq for the development of planetary culture.

This enlarged edition contains an additional new second part, added to include chapters on 'Natural Drift and the Evolution of Culture' and 'The Transition from Nation-State to Noetic Polity' as well as two shorter reflective pieces.

The author is a poet, cultural historian and founder of the Lindisfarne Association. His many books include *Coming into Being: Artifacts and Texts in the Evolution of Consciousness*.

150 pp., £8.95/$17.90, 9781845401337 (pbk.), July 2009, *Societas,* Vol.41

Universities: The Recovery of an Idea (revised second edition)

Gordon Graham

RAE, teaching quality assessment, student course evaluation, modularization – these are all names of innovations in modern British universities. How far do they constitute a significant departure from traditional academic concerns? Using themes from J.H.Newman's *The Idea of a University* as a starting point, this book aims to address these questions.

'It is extraordinary how much Graham has managed to say (and so well) in a short book.' **Alasdair MacIntyre**

£8.95/$17.90, 9781845401276 (pbk), *Societas* V.1

God in Us: A Case for Christian Humanism

Anthony Freeman

God In Us is a radical representation of the Christian faith for the 21st century. Following the example of the Old Testament prophets and the first-century Christians it overturns received ideas about God. God is not an invisible person 'out there' somewhere, but lives in the human heart and mind as 'the sum of all our values and ideals' guiding and inspiring our lives.

The Revd. Anthony Freeman was dismissed from his parish for publishing this book, but remains a priest in the Church of England.

'Brilliantly lucid.' *Philosophy Now*

'A brave and very well-written book' *The Freethinker*

£8.95/$17.90, 9780907845171 (pbk), *Societas* V.2

The Case Against the Democratic State

Gordon Graham

This essay contends that the gross imbalance of power in the modern state is in need of justification and that democracy simply masks this need with the illusion of popular sovereignty. The book points out the emptiness of slogans like 'power to the people', as individual votes do not affect the outcome of elections, but concludes that democracy can contribute to civic education.

'Challenges the reigning orthodoxy'. *Mises Review*

'Political philosophy in the best analytic tradition... scholarly, clear, and it does not require a professional philosopher to understand it' *Philosophy Now*

'An excellent candidate for inclusion on an undergraduate syllabus.' *Independent Review*

£8.95/$17.90, 9780907845386 (pbk), *Societas* V.3

The Last Prime Minister

Graham Allen MP

This book shows how Britain has acquired an executive presidency by stealth. It is the first ever attempt to codify the Prime Minister's powers, many hidden in the mysteries of the royal prerogative. This timely second edition takes in new issues, including Parliament's impotence over Iraq.

'Iconoclastic, stimulating and well-argued.' **Vernon Bogdanor**, *Times Higher Education Supplement*

'Well-informed and truly alarming.' **Peter Hennessy**

'Should be read by anybody interested in the constitution.' **Anthony King**

£8.95/$17.90, 9780907845416 (pbk), *Societas* V.4

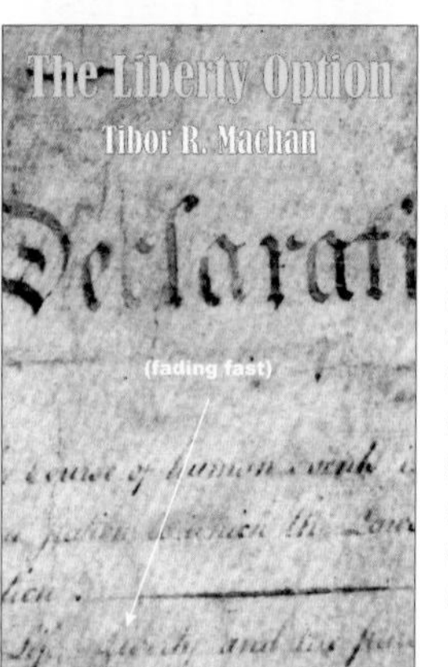

The Liberty Option

Tibor R. Machan

*The Liberty Optio*n advances the idea that it is the society organised on classical liberal principles that serves justice best, leads to prosperity and encourages the greatest measure of individual virtue. The book contrasts this Lockean ideal with the various statist alternatives, defends it against its communitarian critics and lays out some of its more significant policy implications. The author teaches ethics at Chapman University. His books on classical liberal theory include *Classical Individualism* (Routledge, 1998).

£8.95/$17.90, 9780907845638 (pbk), *Societas* V.5

Democracy, Fascism & the New World Order

Ivo Mosley

Growing up as the grandson of Sir Oswald, the 1930s blackshirt leader, made Ivo Mosley consider fascism with a deep and acutely personal interest. Whereas conventional wisdom sets up democracy and fascism as opposites, to ancient political theorists democracy had an innate tendency to lead to extreme populist government, and provided unscrupulous demagogues with the ideal opportunity to seize power. In *Democracy, Fascism and the New World Order* Mosley argues that totalitarian regimes may well be the logical outcome of unfettered mass democracy.

'Brings a passionate reasoning to the analysis'. *Daily Mail*

'Read Mosley's, in many ways, excellent book. But read it critically.' **Edward Ingram**, *Philosophy Now*

£8.95/$17.90, 9780907845645 (pbk), *Societas* V.6

Off With Their Wigs!

Charles Banner and Alexander Deane

On June 12, 2003, a press release concerning a Cabinet reshuffle declared as a footnote that the ancient office of Lord Chancellor was to be abolished and that a new supreme court would replace the House of Lords as the highest appeal court. This book critically analyses the Government's proposals and looks at the various alternative models for appointing judges and for a new court of final appeal.

'A cogently argued critique.' *Commonwealth Lawyer*

£8.95/$17.90, 9780907845843 (pbk), *Societas* V.7

The Modernisation Imperative

Bruce Charlton & Peter Andras

Modernisation gets a bad press in the UK, and is blamed for increasing materialism, moral fragmentation, the dumbing-down of public life, declining educational standards, occupational insecurity and rampant managerialism. But modernisation is preferable to the likely alternative of lapsing back towards a 'medieval' world of static, hierarchical and coercive societies – the many and serious criticisms of modernisation should be seen as specific problems relating to a process that is broadly beneficial for most of the people, most of the time.

'A powerful and new analysis'. **Matt Ridley**

£8.95/$17.90, 9780907845522 (pbk), *Societas* V.8

Self and Society, *William Irwin Thompson*

£8.95/$17.90, 9780907845829 (pbk), *Societas* V.9
now superceded by Vol.41 (see above, p.S6)

The Party's Over

Keith Sutherland

This book questions the role of the party in the post-ideological age and concludes that government ministers should be appointed by headhunters and held to account by a parliament selected by lot.

'Sutherland's model of citizen's juries ought to have much greater appeal to progressive Britain.' *Observer*

'An extremely valuable contribution.' *Tribune*

'A political essay in the best tradition – shrewd, erudite, polemical, partisan, mischievous and highly topical.' *Contemporary Political Theory*

£8.95/$17.90, 9780907845515 (pbk), *Societas* V.10

Our Last Great Illusion

Rob Weatherill

This book aims to refute, primarily through the prism of modern psychoanalysis and postmodern theory, the notion of a return to nature, to holism, or to a pre-Cartesian ideal of harmony and integration. Far from helping people, therapy culture's utopian solutions may be a cynical distraction, creating delusions of hope. Yet solutions proliferate in the free market; this is why therapy is our last great illusion. The author is a psychoanalytic psychotherapist and lecturer, Trinity College, Dublin.

'Challenging, but well worth the engagement.' *Network*

£8.95/$17.90, 9780907845959 (pbk), *Societas* V.11

The Snake that Swallowed its Tail

Mark Garnett

Liberal values are the hallmark of a civilised society, but depend on an optimistic view of the human condition, Stripped of this essential ingredient, liberalism has become a hollow abstraction. Tracing its effects through the media, politics and the public services, the book argues that hollowed-out liberalism has helped to produce our present discontent.

'This arresting account will be read with profit by anyone interested in the role of ideas in politics.' **John Gray**, *New Statesman*

'A spirited polemic addressing the malaise of British politics.' **Michael Freeden**, *The European Legacy*

£8.95/$17.90, 9780907845881 (pbk), *Societas* V.12

Why the Mind is Not a Computer

Raymond Tallis

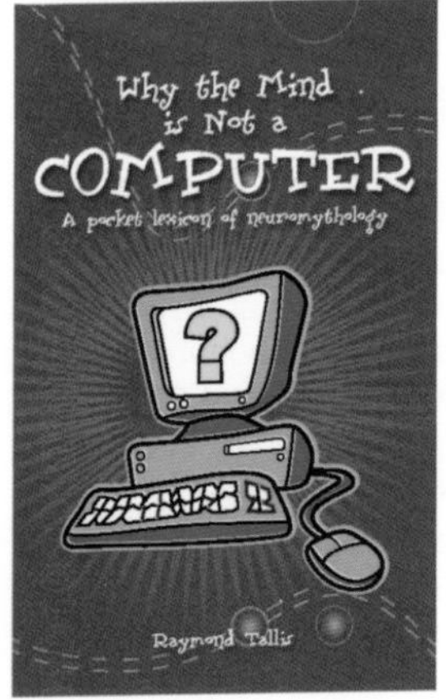

The equation 'Mind = Machine' is false. This pocket lexicon of 'neuromythology' shows why. Taking a series of keywords such as calculation, language, information and memory, Professor Tallis shows how their misuse has a misled a generation. First of all these words were used literally in the description of the human mind. Then computer scientists applied them metaphorically to the workings of machines. And finally the use of the terms was called as evidence of artificial intelligence in machines *and* the computational nature of thought.

'A splendid exception to the helpless specialisation of our age' **Mary Midgley**, *THES*

'A work of radical clarity.' *J. Consciousness Studies*

£8.95/$17.90, 9780907845942 (pbk), *Societas* V.13

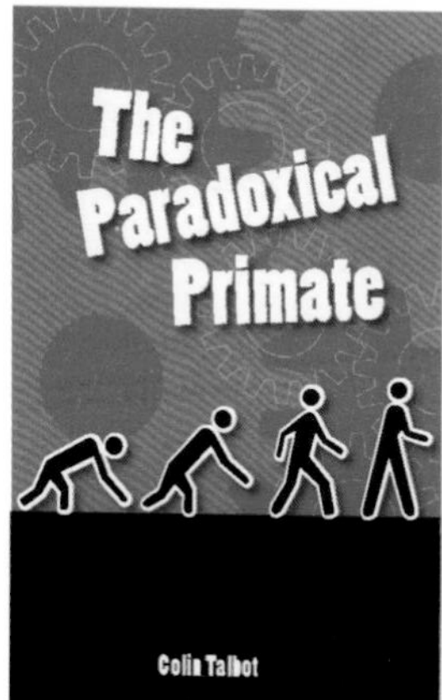

The Paradoxical Primate

Colin Talbot

This book seeks to explain how human beings can be so malleable, yet have an inherited set of instincts. When E.O. Wilson's *Consilience* made a plea for greater integration, it was assumed that the traffic would be from physical to human science. Talbot reverses this assumption and reviews some of the most innovative developments in evolutionary psychology, ethology and behavioural genetics.

'Talbot's ambition is admirable...a framework that can simultaneously encompass individualism and concern for collective wellbeing.' *Public* (The Guardian)

£8.95/$17.90, 9780907845850 (pbk), *Societas* V.14

Tony Blair and the Ideal Type

J.H. Grainger

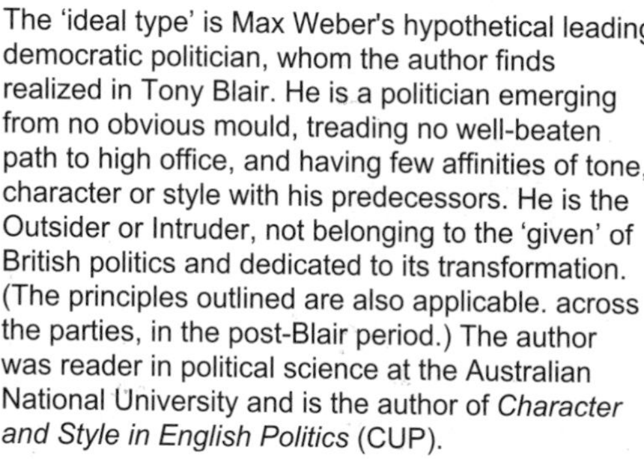

The 'ideal type' is Max Weber's hypothetical leading democratic politician, whom the author finds realized in Tony Blair. He is a politician emerging from no obvious mould, treading no well-beaten path to high office, and having few affinities of tone, character or style with his predecessors. He is the Outsider or Intruder, not belonging to the 'given' of British politics and dedicated to its transformation. (The principles outlined are also applicable. across the parties, in the post-Blair period.) The author was reader in political science at the Australian National University and is the author of *Character and Style in English Politics* (CUP).

'A brilliant essay.' **Simon Jenkins**, *Sunday Times*

'A scintillating case of the higher rudeness.' *Guardian*

£8.95/$17.90, 9781845400248 (pbk), *Societas* V.15

The Great Abdication

Alex Deane

According to Deane, Britain's middle class has abstained from its responsibility to uphold societal values, resulting in the collapse of our society's norms and standards. The middle classes must reinstate themselves as arbiters of morality, be unafraid to judge their fellow men, and follow through with the condemnation that follows when individuals sin against common values.

'[Deane] thinks there is still an element in the population which has traditional middle-class values. Well, maybe.' **George Wedd**, *Contemporary Review*

£8.95/$17.90, 9780907845973 (pbk), *Societas* V.16

Who's Afraid of a European Constitution?

Neil MacCormick

This book discusses how the EU Constitution was drafted, whether it promised any enhancement of democracy in the EU and whether it implied that the EU is becoming a superstate. The arguments are equally of interest regarding the EU Reform Treaty.

Sir Neil MacCormick is professor of public law at Edinburgh University. He was an MEP and a member of the Convention on the Future of Europe.

£8.95/$17.90, 9781845392 (pbk), *Societas* V.17

Darwinian Conservatism

Larry Arnhart

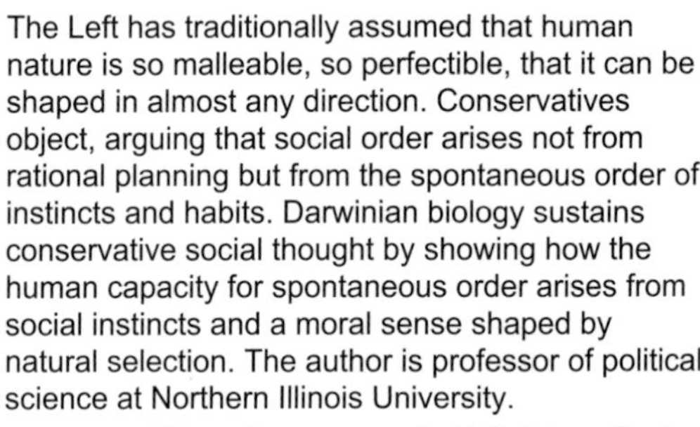

The Left has traditionally assumed that human nature is so malleable, so perfectible, that it can be shaped in almost any direction. Conservatives object, arguing that social order arises not from rational planning but from the spontaneous order of instincts and habits. Darwinian biology sustains conservative social thought by showing how the human capacity for spontaneous order arises from social instincts and a moral sense shaped by natural selection. The author is professor of political science at Northern Illinois University.

'Strongly recommended.' *Salisbury Review*

'An excellect book.' **Anthony Flew**, *Right Now!*

'Conservative critics of Darwin ignore Arnhart at their own peril.' *Review of Politics*

96 pp., £8.95/$17.90, 9780907845997 (pbk.), *Societas,* Vol. 18

Doing Less With Less: Making Britain More Secure

Paul Robinson

Notwithstanding the rhetoric of the 'war on terror', the world is now a far safer place. However, armed forces designed for the Cold War encourage global interference through pre-emption and other forms of military interventionism. We would be safer with less. The author, an ex-army officer, is assistant director of the Centre for Security Studies at Hull University.

'Robinson's criticisms need to be answered.' **Tim Garden**, *RUSI Journal*

'The arguments in this thesis should be acknowledged by the MOD.' **Major General Patrick Cordingley DSO**

£8.95/$17.90, 9781845400422 (pbk), *Societas* V.19

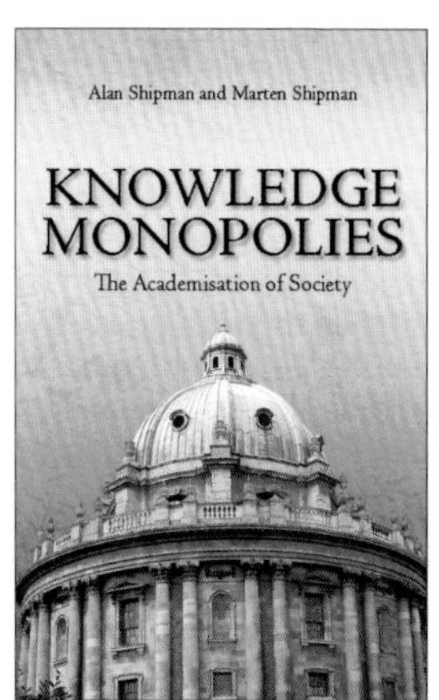

Knowledge Monopolies

Alan Shipman & Marten Shipman

Historians and sociologists chart the *consequences* of the expansion of knowledge; philosophers of science examine the *causes*. This book bridges the gap. The focus is on the paradox whereby, as the general public becomes better educated to live and work with knowledge, the 'academy' increases its intellectual distance, so that the nature of reality becomes more rather than less obscure.

'A deep and searching look at the successes and failures of higher education.' *Commonwealth Lawyer*

'A must read.' *Public* (The Guardian)

£8.95/$17.90, 9781845400286 (pbk), *Societas* V.20

The Referendum Roundabout

Kieron O'Hara

A lively and sharp critique of the role of the referendum in modern British politics. The 1975 vote on Europe is the lens to focus the subject, and the controversy over the referendum on the European constitution is also in the author's sights.

The author is a senior research fellow at the University of Southampton and author of *Plato and the Internet*, *Trust: From Socrates to Spin* and *After Blair: Conservatism Beyond Thatcher* (2005).

£8.95/$17.90, 9781845400408 (pbk), *Societas* V.21

The Moral Mind

Henry Haslam

The reality and validity of the moral sense took a battering in the last century. Materialist trends in philosophy, the decline in religious faith, and a loosening of traditional moral constraints added up to a shift in public attitudes, leaving many people aware of a questioning of moral claims and uneasy with a world that has no place for the morality. Haslam shows how important the moral sense is to the human personality and exposes the weakness in much current thinking that suggests otherwise.

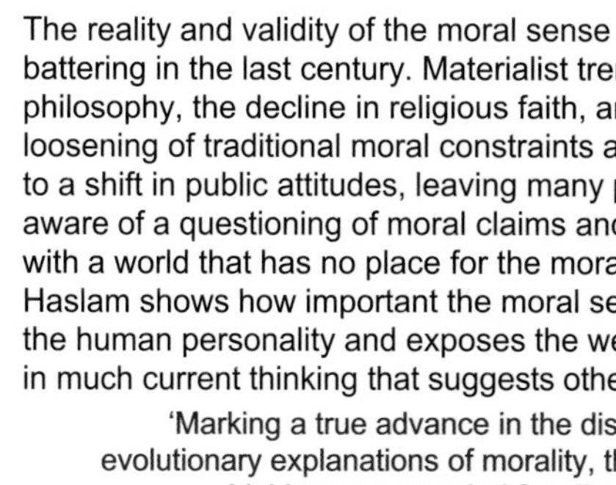

'Marking a true advance in the discussion of evolutionary explanations of morality, this book is highly recommended for all collections.' **David Gordon**, *Library Journal*

'An extremely sensible little book. It says things that are really rather obvious, but which have somehow got forgotten.' **Mary Midgley**

£8.95/$17.90, 9781845400163 (pbk), *Societas* V.22

Putting Morality Back Into Politics *Richard D. Ryder*

Ryder argues that the time has come for public policies to be seen to be based upon moral objectives. Politicians should be expected routinely to justify their policies with open moral argument. In Part I, Ryder sketches an overview of contemporary political philosophy as it relates to the moral basis for politics, and Part 2 suggests a way of putting morality back into politics, along with a clearer emphasis upon scientific evidence. Trained as a psychologist, the author has also been a political lobbyist, mostly in relation to animal welfare.

£8.95/$17.90, 9781845400477 (pbk), *Societas* V.23

Village Democracy

John Papworth

'A civilisation that genuinely reflects all that human beings long for and aspire to can only be created on the basis of each person's freely acknowledged power to decide on each of the many questions that affect his life.' In the forty years since he wrote those words in the first issue of his journal *Resurgence*, John Papworth has not wavered from that belief. This latest book passionately restates his argument for radical decentralisation.

'If we are to stand any chance of surviving we need to heed Papworth's call for decentralisation.'
Zac Goldsmith, *The Ecologist*

£8.95/$17.90, 9781845400644 (pbk), *Societas* V.24

Debating Humanism

Dolan Cummings (ed.)

Broadly speaking, the humanist tradition is one in which it is we as human beings who decide for ourselves what is best for us, and are responsible for shaping our own societies. For humanists, then, debate is all the more important, not least at a time when there is discussion about the unexpected return of religion as a political force. This collection of essays follows the Institute of Ideas' inaugural 2005 Battle of Ideas festival. Contributors include Josie Appleton, Simon Blackburn, Robert Brecher, Andrew Copson, Dylan Evans, Revd. Anthony Freeman, Frank Furedi, A.C. Grayling, Dennis Hayes, Elisabeth Lasch-Quinn, Kenan Malik and Daphne Patai.

£8.95/$17.90, 9781845400699 (pbk), *Societas* V.25

The Right Road to Radical Freedom *Tibor R. Machan*

This work focuses on the topic of free will – do we as individual human beings choose our conduct, at least partly independently, freely? He comes down on the side of libertarians who answer Yes, and scorns the compatibilism of philosophers like Daniel Dennett, who try to rescue some kind of freedom from a physically determined universe. From here he moves on to apply his belief in radical freedom to areas of life such as religion, politics, and morality, tackling subjects as diverse as taxation, private property, justice and the welfare state.

£8.95/$17.90, 9781845400187 (pbk), *Societas* V.26

Paradoxes of Power: Reflections on the Thatcher Interlude

Sir Alfred Sherman

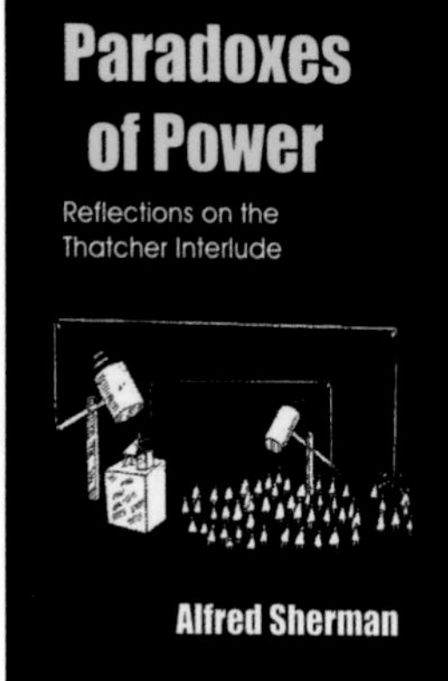

In her memoirs Lady Thatcher herself pays tribute to her former adviser's 'brilliance', the 'force and clarity of his mind', his 'breadth of reading and his skills as a ruthless polemicist'. She credits him with a central role in her achievements. Born in 1919 in London's East End, until 1948 Sherman was a Communist and fought in the Spanish Civil War. But he ended up a free-market crusader.

'These reflections by Thatcherism's inventor are necessary reading.' **John Hoskyns**, *Salisbury Review*

£8.95/$17.90, 9781845400927 (pbk), *Societas* V.27

Public Health & Globalisation

Iain Brassington

This book claims that the NHS is morally indefensible. There is a good moral case in favour of a *public* health service, but these arguments do not point towards a *national* health service, but to something that looks far more like a *transnational* health service. Drawing on Peter Singer's famous arguments in favour of a duty of rescue, the author argues that the cost of the NHS is unjustifiable. If we accept a duty to save lives when the required sacrifice is small, then we ought also to accept sacrifices in the NHS in favour of foreign aid. This does not imply that the NHS is wrong; just that it is wrong to spend large amounts on one person in Britain when we could save more lives elsewhere.

£8.95/$17.90, 9781845400798 (pbk), *Societas* V.28

Why Spirituality is Difficult for Westerners *David Hay*

Zoologist David Hay holds that religious or spiritual awareness is biologically natural to the human species and has been selected for in organic evolution because it has survival value. Although naturalistic, this hypothesis is not intended to be reductionist. Indeed, it implies that all people have a spiritual life. This book describes the historical and economic context of European secularism, and considers recent developments in neurophysiology of the brain as it relates to religious experience.

£8.95/$17.90, 9781845400484 (pbk), *Societas* V.29

Earthy Realism: The Meaning of GAIA

Mary Midgley (ed.)

GAIA, named after the ancient Greek mother-goddess, is the notion that the Earth and the life on it form an active, self-maintaining whole. It has a *scientific* side, as shown by the new university departments of earth science which bring biology and geology together to study the continuity of the cycle. It also has a visionary or *spiritual* aspect. What the contributors to this book believe is needed is to bring these two angles together. With global warming now an accepted fact, the lessons of GAIA have never been more relevant and urgent. Foreword by James Lovelock.

£8.95/$17.90, 9781845400804 (pbk), *Societas* V.30

Joseph Conrad Today

Kieron O'Hara

This book argues that the novelist Joseph Conrad's work speaks directly to us in a way that none of his contemporaries can. Conrad's scepticism, pessimism, emphasis on the importance and fragility of community, and the difficulties of escaping our history are important tools for understanding the political world in which we live. He is prepared to face a future where progress is not inevitable, where actions have unintended consequences, and where we cannot know the contexts in which we act. The result can hardly be called a political programme, but Conrad's work is clearly suggestive of a sceptical conservatism of the sort described by the author in his 2005 book *After Blair: Conservatism Beyond Thatcher.*

£8.95/$17.90, 9781845400668 (pbk.), *Societas* V.31